FAITH UNDER FIRE

& THE REVOLUTIONS IN EASTERN EUROPE

By Augustin Hedberg

An Eyewitness
to the Victory of
the Human Spirit

Based on Transcripts
from the Film
Faith Under Fire

STURGES PUBLISHING • PRINCETON • NEW JERSEY

Library of Congress Catalog Card Number
Faith Under Fire & the Revolutions in Eastern Europe
By Augustin Hedberg
An Eyewitness to the Victory of the Human Spirit
Based on Edited Transcripts of Interviews Conducted by
DeWitt Sage for Faith Under Fire

0–936373–04–0

91-75072
CIP

Manufactured in the United States
First Edition

FAITH UNDER FIRE

CONTENTS

PREFACE   vii

ACKNOWLEDGEMENTS   xv

CZECHOSLOVAKIA

CHAPTER 1   President Havel   3

CHAPTER 2   Father Maly   11

CHAPTER 3   Professor Hejdánek   21

CHAPTER 4   Father Kansky   29

CHAPTER 5   Mr. Jelinek   41

CHAPTER 6   Cardinal Korec   53

CHAPTER 7   Dean Trojan   63

CHAPTER 8   Pastor Kocáb   73

CHAPTER 9   Töpfer the Actor   83

POLAND

CHAPTER 10   Bujak the Worker   95

CHAPTER 11   Popieluszko's Mother   103

CHAPTER 12   Brother Giertych   108

CHAPTER 13   Mr. Kakol   125

CHAPTER 14   Father Czajkowski   131

CHAPTER 15   Father Tischner   141

CHAPTER 16   Gal the Shepherd   151

THE GERMAN ANTECEDENT

CHAPTER 17   Professor Bethge   157

FAITH
UNDER
FIRE

Dr. Hollis D. Hedberg (1903–1988), at right, on his way to the Technical College with a Czech colleague in occupied Prague, August, 1968.

PREFACE

I first set foot in Prague, the city in which many of the events in this book take place, on August 20, 1968. I arrived only hours before 200,000 Warsaw Pact soldiers, and I left four days later, greatly changed. I was then a recently radicalized youth, fresh from the uproarious student revolution that took place that April on the campus of Columbia University and quickly spread through America's other high-rent academic neighborhoods.

These were heady days in the United States. At college, we read Marx, Engels, Fourier, Marcuse, Ortega, Paul Goodman and Norman O. Brown. The dark side of Western capitalism was laid bare on the blackboard before us by the professorate. I do not suggest that the university was then a "hotbed of Marxism." We also read Hume, Burke, Hobbes and Dr. Johnson. But for some reason, the adversaries of capitalism, in the hypothetical context of the classroom, seemed the more intriguing. To many of us, the drawing-board logic of Marxism seemed unassailable. Even inevitable.

Students would sometimes ask why Marxism seemed often to take the form of the unpleasant totalitarian governments in Eastern Europe and elsewhere around the world, or ask why restrictions on the practice of religion, free travel, and free speech were necessary. There were several stock answers. Such measures were necessary, one argument went, to keep these systems unpolluted by the vices of capitalism. Or that the workers in those countries could not be expected to fully appreciate the beauty of such ideas and thus they had to be imposed from above for the benefit of all. Or sometimes the famous Freudian omelet would be invoked, which to make, required unfortunately the breaking of some eggs.

Since none of us was currently being cracked on the edge of the pan–nor, for that matter were any of the teachers–the whole idea of Marxism and state communism seemed to be some distant yet terribly important social experiment that could be followed in little journals and scholarly screeds. By the time it inexorably arrived on our shores, it surely would have ironed out its infelicities. There was another argument that suggested that the repressive nature of many Communist governments was actually the results of economic and military pressures put on those countries by our own. If we would let up, they would let up. So the argument went. There we sat, smart kids, by someone's measure, happy to find some causal connection between our country's building of a battleship and the quiet suffering of people in Eastern Europe. The more tenuous the connection, the better we liked it.

Anyway, the times were distracting enough. America in 1968 was plugged in, drugged out and hot for change. Everything was possible, nothing seemed necessary. Only change counted. But what change exactly, no one had a clue. Outside the classroom window, "Burn, baby, burn," echoed in the streets. And, perhaps because we guessed that we might be among the babies marked to burn, we were happy to set fires everywhere else.

My roommate went to jail with 700 other students for occupying the Chancellor's office at Columbia. I knew a girl who was fabricating bombs in her parents' townhouse. The New York City police stormed into a crowd of students and faculty on the Columbia campus and laid about themselves, rather randomly, with their nightsticks. I remember fleeing down Broadway with about a thousand other people, the mounted police clattering behind us on the iron freight-elevator plates in the sidewalk, straining to get their truncheons on our well-read heads. I thought I had seen everything.

Truly, I had seen nothing. That summer, as Columbia smoldered in the rubble left by the student uprising, I went to Prague. My father, a professor of geology at Princeton, had been invited to represent the United States at the International Geological Congress held that year in Prague. He had arranged for my mother, my sister and myself to enter Czechoslovakia with him. I traveled about Europe for a few weeks and then, on August 19th, took the train from Vienna to Prague to meet my family who had been in the city for several days.

"Svoboda!" said the Czech cabdriver, upon learning I was an American, and swinging around with a big grin in the middle of traffic. He pointed to me and said "Svoboda" again as if it were my name. Then he tapped himself on the chest, swept an arm out as if to indicate the whole city, and said the word again. It meant "freedom," I later learned, and the cabdriver, like everyone in Prague, was drunk with the possibilities of that conjuring word.

That spring the government of Alexander Dubcek had, to the amazement of the whole world, and to the Czechs themselves, slipped loose from its hard-line Soviet overseers in Moscow. The Czechs were in a state of collective rapture that was evident on every face in the city. The streets hummed with excitement. People sang aloud, and greeted everyone they met like old friends. Backs were slapped, hands extended, and Prague, that dark city of gargoyles and knobby spires, beamed like a jewel in the iron crown of Eastern Europe.

The next morning Warsaw Pact troops took the city. They arrived that night by air, transport after transport, from bases in the Soviet Union and other Bloc countries. The Prague airport was seized, and Russian fighters streaked over the town spraying the sky with tracers to discourage the Czechs from any thoughts of resistance. On the morning of August 21, columns of tanks entered the city pulverizing the curbs with their treads and rotating their cannons at the groups of citizens that watched with horror. Machine gun fire rattled sporadically throughout the day, and people died. All contact with the world was cut off. Any show of protest or resistance was quickly neutralized. In the streets Czech men and women wept openly as their parks and squares filled up with tanks and soldiers.

A common characterization of totalitarianism is that it can be precise and efficient in detail while being, at the same time, wildly absurd and nonsensical from any larger frame of reference. It soon became clear that many of these soldiers, most of them in their teens, who had so efficiently paralyzed the city of Prague, in fact, had no idea where they were. Worse, those who did, had somehow been informed that they would be greeted as heroes or liberators. The common scene was to see several tanks wheel into a quiet public park, crush a few curbstones, plow down some shrubbery and grind to a halt. Hatch lids would fly open and soldiers would scramble out wearing broad triumphal smiles only to be met with the stony, tearful faces of the Czechs who were witnessing the devastation of their city and their dreams.

Personally, I was gripped with a terror I had never before imagined. The overwhelming power and thoroughness of the occupation, the omnipresence of ordnance and the menacing appearance of strike-force soldiers in every bush inspired in me a shameful desire to simply get out. Rumors spread through the city like wind, and panic was barely contained. NATO forces were supposed to be massing at the German border for an assault on the city. The Soviet Union, one story had it, was now in the hands of an insane military dictator bent on pushing its borders westward. Apocalyptic war was about to ignite in Prague.

Many Western visitors did flee. The invaders were not eager to have their invasion witnessed and were as quickly as possible clearing the city of Americans and other foreigners. In our hotel at the time was a Hollywood film crew, in Prague to make the movie, "The Bridge at Remagen." The Americans in the crew, including stars whose names were household words in the States, had been granted permission to take their buses and equipment back to Western Europe. But only the Americans. It is hard to forget the scene that took place in front of the hotel when several British crew members were informed that, for diplomatic reasons, they were not to be included in the escape. One elderly Englishman, a cinematographer, was ejected from the bus and was left clutching hysterically at the rubber gaskets on the bus door as my countrymen, who were there to portray the war heroes of another time, made their flight for freedom.

Svoboda. How little I, they, or my friends and my professors back in the U.S. knew about the frailty of this happy word. But I would have probably been on the bus with the actors, had it not been for my father. He was going no where. As he saw it, the Czech government had invited him to represent his country at an international meeting of scientists and, until the Czechs themselves asked him to leave, he would stay. For three days, he trudged off each morning and threaded his way through the tanks between the hotel and the Technical College where the Congress was being held. The Congress nervously continued. Papers were presented. International scientific standards were agreed upon. And in time the Czech scientists, whether under pressure from Moscow or in desperation, brought the proceedings to an end.

On August 23rd, I went to hear my father deliver a final statement on behalf of the American delegation to a greatly diminished audience at the Technical College. He assured the Czechs that their efforts to keep the Congress going while their city was being held at gunpoint were not in vain. And he made it clear that their message would be passed abroad through their fellow scientists. I shall never forget his example of courage and patriotism, and it is in his memory that I have undertaken the preparation and annotation of the interviews in this book, many of which are with men and women, most of them priests or ministers, who have endured for decades a curtailment of freedom that would be unthinkable in the context of American life.

"Tell everything you've seen here," were the parting words of the Czechs when we left the broken city by train the day after the Geological Congress was closed. Seven hours later we were at the U.S. Army base in Nuremberg, West Germany, and an attractive soldier with the hard-to-forget name of Dixie Star served us coffee and donuts and welcomed us back to the "free world." A week earlier I might have bristled at that characterization, which would have to account for the inequalities and corruptions that were clearly a part of our system. But it was in no diminution of the gravity of those imperfections that I resolved then to always act and vote, in whatever way possible, to harrow and strangle that other system that had so brutally bled the Czechs of their basic human rights.

Today, in 1992, more than two decades after the occupation of Prague, that inhumane system has been brought down. I personally believe its fall is the result of forces acting on it from without and from within. Only dreamers in a class with those who strove decades ago to excuse the cruelty of communism as a necessary means to a good end could possible imagine that Western military and economic pressure were not critical factors in the fall of the Iron Curtain. But these alone would not have been enough.

What the Communist governments of Eastern Europe failed to take into account when they proposed to reconstitute human existence in the light of an intellectual ideal was human nature itself. Some parts of this nature—the will to speak freely, to believe in God, to practice that belief communally, the tension between conscience and action, and the hatred of tyranny—seem to press upward on any lid closed over them. They will appear in the most unlikely places. And men and women, who even to themselves would seem to be the most unlikely vehicles of these expressions, will rise against unthinkable odds to assert these rights.

This is a book of telling. There is no analysis here. No explanation or political perspective. The interviews were conducted by the filmmaker, DeWitt L. Sage, who visited Eastern Europe during the spring and summer of 1991 under a grant from the Lilly Endowment and WNET-13 of New York. He went to explore the role of the church—the role of faith and conscience—in the unwinding of Communist control over Eastern Europe. The result of his visit is the remarkable television documentary, *Faith Under Fire*. In Poland and in Czechoslovakia, he interviewed priests, pastors, church leaders, activists, and former government bureaucrats, asking them questions such as these. What role did the church play in the overthrow of totalitarianism? What role did you play? When were you most afraid? What did you do?

Their answers, which came to me in the form of 700 pages of unedited manuscripts, tell a vivid story of the tension between courage and compromise, and the variety of human reactions to that challenge. Readers of this book must understand that these interviews were conducted to obtain brief, powerful testimonies for inclusion in the film. In most cases the interviewer spoke through an interpreter and the answers were simultaneously translated in front of the rolling camera. Questions were often repeated several times to sharpen the answers, and the transcripts that resulted were in broken English and, often, unintelligible.

My job has been to piece together the main themes of each interview and to edit the phrasing and vocabulary into an abridged form that would lend itself to publication. My obvious guidelines in creating publishable renditions of these interview have been to never embellish, emotionalize, or exaggerate the words of the subjects. Interpretation has, at times, been a necessary factor in extracting a clear meaning from certain passages. And in some instances, the task of rendering the raw language of translation into idiomatic English may have bent the exact intent of those being interviewed. But that is a liability of any translation or rephrasing.

Each interview, as it appears here, has been read for accuracy by bilingual consultants who were present during the filming. And historical, biographical and explicative annotations are provided in the margin where they are deemed necessary. It is easy to read these interviews and praise the martyrs, damn the collaborators, and laugh at the ridiculous excuses of the bureaucrats. A careful reader will quickly see that this reaction misses the point. Heroes and villains are here, but what emerges most powerfully is the banal perniciousness of the spiderweb in which these governments entangled their people. Father Alois Kansky, the young priest who tells here of his own struggle with courage and compromise, also warns us: "Mainly you should not judge. You shouldn't judge people for what they have done from fear, because you don't know anything about it. You didn't live through this."

During the summer after the film was shot, I returned to Czechoslovakia and interviewed many priests, pastors and church members to cross-check the startling stories that are told here. It is my opinion that the accounts in this book are uniformly accurate. And it is my prayer that their like will never need be told again.

AUGUSTIN HEDBERG

ACKNOWLEDGEMENTS

The editor and the publisher wish to thank the following people and institutions for lending their time and resources to the development and completion of this book: photographer Ulli Bonnekamp and his wife Dyanna Taylor, Craig Dykstra and Jim Wind of the Lilly Endowment, Hal Rast of Trinity Press International, Dan Matthews, the Rector of Trinity Wall Street, Ted Landreth, Arnie Labaton of WNET-13, Caren Sturges, Lisa Coffman, Eva Perusic, Ewa Zadryznska, and the Lawrenceville School. The publisher is especially grateful to DeWitt Sage for having made available the unedited transcripts of the film *Faith Under Fire* during its production.

The filmmaker, DeWitt Sage interviewing
Václav Havel, President of Czechoslovakia, for
the documentary film, Faith Under Fire.

I

Czechoslovakia

The President: Fear and the Rise of the Church

In the context of European countries under the control of Communists, this country, I gather, was one of the most conservative and one of the most repressed. Why did this happen?

Yes, I agree with the fact that the local regime in Czechoslovakia was the most conservative. There are several reasons for this. Some go as far back as 40 years to the days after the Communist putsch when the Communist government was installed here and it attempted a high-speed nationalization of what was then a very diverse country. The "Czechoslovak System" was created then. Everything changed in 1968 when a relatively reformist government came to power and attempted to liberalize the

Václav Havel, playwright and author, was one of the original framers of Charter 77. After adding his name to the Czech manifesto of human rights, Havel lived for seven years as an official "enemy of the state." He was interrogated and imprisoned several times. He is today the first elected President of the new Czech and Slovak Federal Republic.

system. When this reform wing of the Communist party was destroyed by the invasion of the Soviet army, tens of thousands of the reformists lost their jobs, and a group of totally incompetent people came to power. They were also totally incompetent morally, and thanks to that an extremely tough bureaucratic centralism was created in our country.

It was different in Hungary and Poland. They had different systems. By the end of the '80s, we were in one of the worst situations of any Communist country.

What were your own mechanisms of survival? How did you arrive personally at a dividing line between action and inaction, conscience and compromise?

T.G. Masaryk (1850-1937), was the first President of Czechoslovakia. Johann Amos Comenius was a 17th-century Moroavian educational reformer. Petr Chelcicky was the 16th-century founder of the Evangelical Church of Czech Brethren.

Before I will answer that question, I should tell you that this idea of non-violent resistance, of tolerant humanism, has quite a long tradition in our country. It will be enough to remind you of President Masaryk, the founder of our modern state. It is enough to remind you of Komenius, Chelcicky and the others.

Charter 77 reconnected with this tradition, with the conception of decisive but non-violent resistance against the totalitarian system. Later, this created the revolution which also had a kind of strange lovable tolerance to it. A peaceful face.

So all this has its historical background. And for me personally, I was all my life trying to live in the spirit of these ideas and in the context of these thoughts. I was always thinking that I should live in this light—as a civic person.

Of course, that person must, as always, compromise. But if I did compromise, the compromises were not deep or basic. I was always trying to create my own philosophy. As it turned out, Charter 77's philosophy was very near to my own. We had to make some compromises. I still have to compromise now as a president.

As far as the form and tactics are concerned, these are really a question of taste and choice of words. They may differ but they really don't touch the essential ideas and values and principles.

How did you deal with fear?

As far as fear is concerned, I must admit I never felt a real fear of the Communist regime. I knew when I made the decision to resist, that I was

Václav Havel

risking some things, and that I was ready to take that risk. It was calculated somehow in my brain and in my behavior.

I was at times nervous. It was difficult to write—to create—not knowing if somebody is going to ring the bell and pick me up and take me to jail. If I could have known, for example, that I would be free for a year, and then, come January 1st, I shall be in prison for a year, and then free after that, then I could plan my work around it. But to take me to jail without letting me finish my work made things very difficult and instilled a kind of fear: fear of loosing my manuscript, fear of not being able to finish something. I was afraid that my plans would collapse. I like to plan things, and I like to know exactly what is ahead of me. But this was not real fear.

The fact that I can be persecuted or that they can search my house or put me in jail, was calculated into my actions and I was ready for it. Real fear, for me was a fear of myself. A fear of my own conscience and a fear of remorse. I was afraid that I would not be able to pass the test. That they were going to catch me and that I was going to say something wrong. It was a paradoxical fear that became the engine that fueled my behavior, which some people called heroic. I do not consider myself heroic or fearless.

I would describe myself as a person who was so afraid of remorse and afraid of God, that he had to act in a way that other people called heroic.

When I look at the footage of Letná Stadium and I see millions of people cheering and yelling, I remember that for a very long time few people dared to speak against the system. What happened? Why, after all those years, did the true emotions come out almost overnight? What triggered it?

This is quite an interesting question. To answer it completely would be to write a book. But I would say two things. Throughout my life I have noticed that society is quite a mysterious thing. It is more mysterious than human existence itself, which is mysterious enough.

Society is mysterious because we never can safely know what its behavior can mean and what is behind it. Now this society is just showing its face to us. We are willing to believe that this face is the true face, the only face, and we can say our nation is a nation of heroes or cowards. But we always forget that this face can lie.

Society has different faces. When we see them we are shocked. There

The demonstration, which took place in November, 1989 at Letná in Prague, was held in support of dissident leaders and the signers of Charter 77. An estimated 600,000 people were present. It marked a key event in the peaceful revolution that resulted in the fall of the Communist government in Czechoslovakia.

are powers in society that are invisible. I remember in 1968, when the Soviet army came to my country, how the whole society was suddenly intelligently and bravely able to resist. It was very interesting. One would not believe that a destroyed, demoralized and apathetic society could perform like this. And after that moment, one would not believe how it all disappeared and how fast that same society showed a different face.

The second thing I have observed is that before the November revolution of 1989 the tension in our society was growing. It was quite clear that sooner or later something had to happen. Perhaps it was not visible to the visitor from the West who came to the hotels and walked in the streets. Maybe he would not notice any tension. But it was in the air. And I could name dozens of examples that would document this fact. In this totalitarian system where there is no opinion—rather, no expression of opinion—still there are facts when something happens in society. There is no free press or means of information. Still strange things can happen and make the snowball which moves and changes everything. Then everyone is surprised. "What happened? Why is it all changing?"

Several times in interviews before the revolution, I was asked why things were changing in Poland and in Hungary or even in the Soviet Union, but here in Czechoslovakia, with its democratic traditions, things are quiet and the system is simply accepted. I would say over and over, "Be careful. You don't know what will happen tomorrow or the day after tomorrow."

We didn't know whether it was going to happen in one week or maybe after a year. We didn't know how it was going to happen. Not I or anyone. But lots of people were predicting that sooner or later something was going to happen. And, you see, it simply happened.

You have said that conscience precedes being, not the other way around, as the Communists believe. And that conscience is the mediator between consciousness and a Higher Order of Being. Could you explain this?

I have to say, even as president, I again and again see that in stereotypical human behavior, human qualities, good or bad, human habits–whatever I am trying to solve–sooner or later I meet the human soul, the most important theme of everything. The first thing is the soul and thought, and only then there is a social happening.

Václav Havel

I saw you in the footage of Letná Stadium with Father Maly, and you looked, to my eyes, to be frightened. What was going on?

If you thought I looked like a scared person, if I was evoking in you this feeling, it was because I felt responsible for the demonstration. It was decisive and it was dangerous also. It could have ended up in a massacre with incredible persecution. It did not have to end up a victory of democracy. Everything depended on this great demonstration. Three quarters of a million people were there and their behavior was not easy to predict. It was a very strange "show." A political show, whatever you want to call it. And I was feeling responsible. I knew how everything can change in that atmosphere. We were directing this show, and we didn't know what was going to happen. And because we didn't know how the atmosphere might change, we didn't know best how to direct it.

By the end everyone was praying with Václav Maly. It was some kind of purification—the turning point in the revolution. I felt responsible for this great demonstration. It was a historic moment in which everything was being decided. If I was nervous, I was nervous as a director is nervous on opening night–not that it was my play, God forbid.

Someone described Father Maly as a kind of miracle who appeared when he was necessary and then went away. How did it happen that Father Maly was so involved at that decisive moment?

I have thought about that several times myself and I will try to write about it. All this strange revolution in Czechoslovakia, which Western journalists describe as the "Velvet Revolution," (a term, by the way, that we neither use nor like) had a very strange form. As a playwright I realize that it combined all the genres of the theater. It was a political tragedy, a burlesque, a drama and a fairy tale. A fairy tale with a happy ending. It happened so fast, so surprisingly fast, that it also looked like a miracle.

In fact, it has a connection with the prediction of St. Agnes of Bohemia. When all the people from the Cathedral came to the demonstration they were recalling her prediction. It was this mystical dimension that a person like Václav Maly, who is a deep believer, was able to feel.

In Poland and in Germany the churches were safe havens for the opposition. Even for atheists and non-believers. Here it seemed that was impossible. And the theater became the forum. Is that true?

On November 17, 1989, thousands of students marched in protest through Wenceslas Square in the heart of Prague. Police attacked the marchers in an effort to prevent the demonstration. The event marked the beginning of the November Revolution, a month of similar civilian defiance of governmental authority.

Daughter of the 13th-century Czech king, Otakar I, St. Agnes of Bohemia founded the first monastic convents in the Kingdom. She is credited with prophesying that the Czech people will always win over evil.

7

First of all, when we are talking about the church in Poland, there is a different tradition. In Poland the church was identical with the idea of the nation, with patriotic ideas. The church was a symbol of Poland.

On the other hand, in our country, during the Austro-Hungarian monarchy, the church was collaborating with this monarchy, and after the creation of the independent state there was much resentment toward the Greek-Catholic church. Thus rose the Czechoslovak church. It has a reformist tradition, but is not as identified with the fight for freedom as the church is in Poland.

Nevertheless, the popularity of the church changed during the last 20 years of Communist dictatorship. Lots of young people became believers. In the ghoulish consumerist communism where people were just searching for things and where there was no higher ideal, it was hard to make any sense of life. Lots of people were searching for some metaphysical security, and the church gained. The church was also quite brave, thanks to Cardinal Tomasek, for example, and thanks to the hidden structure of the illegal orders. The members of Charter 77 had many different roots. So, in the last stages, the church did become part of the fight.

The tendency of the state was to simply manipulate the church. Not to forbid it, but to make it just some kind of slave. Sometimes this was successful, sometimes not.

There was this great petition that about half a million people signed in 1988, I think, asking that bishops be appointed to unoccupied bishoprics. These were simple believers who started to revolt against these manipulations of the so-called church secretaries. This brought the church into the struggle for the freedom of our nations.

And what happened? After 40 years of learning duplicitous behavior, feeling one thing on the inside and acting a different way on the outside. Has that vanished overnight, or is it here and does it need to be dealt with.

I don't understand this question. These habits cannot disappear overnight. Certain habits just persist, but I don't think that this is the most important problem in our society: that people think one thing and say another. Nobody is forcing them to say anything.

The problem is something else. It is that people don't know what to do with freedom. They have forgotten what freedom is. Freedom came

Václav Havel

suddenly for these people who for decades were waiting for it, longing for it. Now, freedom has created confusion. They felt like a prisoner who has been let out of jail and steps onto free ground and doesn't know what to do.

I experienced this myself several times. And sometimes I even feel this perverted feeling that I would like to return to jail, to the place where there is a tough regime. But suddenly now I have to make decisions for myself, and nobody makes the decisions for me. It's a very strange and very depressing situation.

Father Maly, and the Unforeseeable Action of the Human Heart

Tell me please about the legacy of 40 years of communism in Czechoslovakia. How did it affect the spiritual life and the public life of the people?

During those 40 years people in this country were accustomed to living what I must call "the two faced life." For example, our children were taught at home about the events of the year 1968, and about Alexander Dubcek, but simultaneously, they were told, please, keep silent at the school because it could be dangerous for your further studies.

When people cannot express in public what they privately feel, they lose interest in public affairs. Today, nearly three years after November '89, we can still see the consequences of this kind of existence.

Václav Maly, a young Czech priest ordained in 1976, signed Charter 77 and lost his license to practice as a pastor. He earned his living stoking furnaces in hotels and cleaning subway lavatories, yet continued to lead clandestine Bible groups and prepare people for confirmation. In 1989, he led the blessing at the catalytic demonstration at Letná Stadium and has subsequently returned to pastoral duties.

11

What can the church do about this?

Now, this is a big problem because the church must renew its own structures. The church must overcome its ingrained psychology of defense. It has been for these many years in a defensive posture. Now, it must be more offensive.

What I mean is that the church must reintroduce the structures that it has to offer to society. Above all, it must strive to renew the content of certain words which were forbidden. Words, which up to very recently, were not even mentioned. Words like penance, like hope, like forgiveness, like love.

These words lost their very meaning under the ruling structures of the Communist party. They were not spoken, or if they were, they served only to further the needs of those in power. The church must renew the meaning of these words.

Is that happening now?

It is happening, but only very slowly. One must be very patient. Just to remind the population that these words ever existed is a very difficult task.

For example, the word "forgiveness" has a connotation of weakness. To forgive, in the mind of an ordinary citizen today means: I am weak. I have no choice, therefore I must forgive.

But the contrary is true. Forgiveness is the choice to give another chance to a person, to open a new future to him and cleanse him of his past. Therefore, to forgive is to act with force, to create a change, to open eyes to a new reality.

Let's talk about reality and the idea that the church should be rooted in real life. That it should not be something that just happens from ten to eleven on Sunday mornings—as is often the case in the U.S. I'm wondering, how did you decide that you could merge your faith with the reality around you?

Please, I would not like to exaggerate my significance, but I have always lived in a very concrete situation: the steady struggle between the powerful and the powerless. In Czechoslovakia this has meant that anybody who dared to express his own meaning, could be punished,

Václav Maly

could be sentenced. And this was an enormous injustice for all men and women.

I was educated as a Catholic. Therefore, it was clear to me that faith is not simply an ideal which is apart from ordinary life. It must be always incorporated in that life. It must be always there in whatever circumstances I find myself. Therefore, the struggle for justice in the public life was, for me, automatically connected with my faith.

In the public life there existed a circle of lies. When that circle of lies would be interrupted, I understood it as a victory of the truth in the struggle of faith.

Mr. Solzhenitsyn describes this excellently in his famous essay, "To Live in the Truth." He gave concrete examples for ordinary citizens in the Soviet Union. When you are forced to participate in meetings of the Communist party, he said, please don't raise your hand to agree with the lies of the leaders. When you overcome your internal fear, you will begin to see what victory—the internal victory over internal fears—means. When you interrupted the circle of lies in public life, simultaneously something basic happens in the spiritual life.

As a priest, did you ever think that the people of Czechoslovakia had lost their hope? That they had no strength left?

Yes, I would say the main reason that they pretended to agree with the old ideology, was this internal fear. Everyone is afraid of his own faith. But it is very important to confess it, and not to lie before one's faith. The worst consequence of the ideology that was forced on us was that people started to lie before their own faith. They apologized. They explained their collaboration with the state ideology as simply the best thing to do to survive. But the main thing is not simply to survive. The main thing is to give to life a sense, a sense...

A sense of?

A sense of human dignity. I have learned that it is possible to exhaust the dignity of man under certain living standards. When a person can decide freely, he is really a free human being. When he is forced to only one decision, he is not. Even if he can just see the possible perspectives of his life, he will be less tempted to escape from reality, and may even choose to change reality.

When I look at faces at Letná Stadium, hundreds of thousands, I wonder, how could that feeling have been kept under wraps for so many years, and then suddenly explode? What does it mean that it was there so long, so quietly?

What happened at Letná Stadium and Wenceslas Square during the events of November 1989 is for me, a wonder, a miracle. One can try to analyze the behavior of people politically. But I would say people were lucky that, finally, they could break out,that they could stop this two-faced life. Despite the fact that they behaved in that way, they felt it wasn't right. And, simultaneously, they felt a burden on their shoulders that they must no longer carry. And they were lucky that the words they used could receive there own true meaning again.

It is very hard for anyone to say, in general, the character of this nation is this or is that. A human being is simultaneously what he shows on the surface, and also he is a mystery. One can never foresee the action of the human heart.

Was the act of speaking out dangerous? Did you ever worry about how far you would dare to go?

I was once beaten during an interrogation by the secret police, so obviously I felt fear at the beginning of the November events. To overcome this fear I focused on the awareness that I would be serving the good of the society. I don't struggle for my personal victory, my personal career. Matters of career were irrelevant. In this light, there were only two possibilities: either to win, or to be defeated. Defeat meant prison for 14 or 20 years. But there were only two choices.

Let me ask you about the licensing of priests. The idea of a pastor or a priest having to get a license from the state is unimaginable to a lot of people in the world.

The law controlling the relation between the church and the state was written in 1949. Originally it was intended as a control on the financial matters of the church. The state had confiscated all church property after the war but pledged to pay priests for their activities. Priests had to be licensed in order to be paid. Every priest, not only Catholic priests, had to have a state license from its District Committee of the Party.

Václav Maly

Gradually, however, the state spread this control beyond financial matters, and into the realm of spiritual activities. You see this license could be taken away at any time by the Secretary of the District Committee. No reason for its suspension had to be cited.

Under this system priests were fully at the mercy of the secretaries for church affairs as far as their public activities were concerned. And these secretaries, of course, were connected to the secret police. The actions of every priest were monitored not only by the Party secretary of church affairs, but also by a special team of secret policemen.

By the very nature of his profession, a good priest will attract people. If a priest was observed to attract or influence the people around him— particularly children—he could expect to be replaced, or lose his state license.

For example, I was prevented from working in public in the City of Prague during the last eleven years of Communist rule. When a priest has a state license, he can say holy masses only in his church. If he wanted to say a holy mass in another church, he had to have a special state license. In this way spiritual activities were limited.

In Germany and in Poland, but especially in Germany, the church was able to provide at least a safe roof under which opposition groups could meet. In Poland, the church provided a nursing ground for Solidarity. What about the Czech church?

Sorry, it wasn't the case here. The pressure on the church in Czechoslovakia was the most brutal among the so-called socialist states. The churches here had to concentrate, above all, on holding on to their own structure. The Catholic church, you must remember, had no bishops. Our bishops—the best ones—were detained and imprisoned for many years. The male and female orders were abolished.

The church was practically without leadership. It had no eye for public affairs. It tried to get its believers to strengthen their awareness that they must live together—that the faith isn't only a matter of individual life, but it is a matter of a community.

Opposition groups arose beside the churches. In certain individuals, opposition to the government was connected with the church. Christians were very much engaged in groups like Charter 77 or the Committee for the Defense of the Unjustly Persecuted or the Czechoslovak Helsinki Committee and the Independent Peace Movement. But this connection between the church and the opposition was only through individuals. It wasn't an official connection between the church structures and the structures of those groups.

Why do you think that the control of the church was so much more brutal here than, say, in Poland?

No, please, I would have to write a book about it, because it is a very complicated question. But I would say that the Communists in Czechoslovakia had particularly fertile soil for their ideology. The Communists promised changes in social structures. When they started to rule, they had the support of at least of half of our society. Even in the last free elections in 1946 they won in Bohemia. Half of the voters were already leftists. If I could say it so. Because the tradition of social democracy was entrenched here from the past century, there was an existing bias against Christianity and, unlike in Poland, against the Catholic church.

Is it too naive a hope that, after these long years of duplicity, a nation can be founded on moral principle?

I am very optimistic, but the situation is a little complicated. One observes the current satisfaction with political and economic changes. However there is also great attention to moral values. And, here the voice of Václav Havel is very important. Our society is still deeply ill morally, and Václav Havel addresses this matter.

One cannot expect an instant moral recovery. But thank God that Václav Havel has started the process. Havel has shown us that it is necessary to base politics on moral values. That politics is not solely a matter of power, only a strategy of political opinions, but it must be based on respect for human beings.

Your license was taken away. Why?

It's amazing but even now I don't know exactly why my state license was taken away. As I mentioned earlier, the state secretaries were not required to give specific reasons for the taking of state licenses. It was only suggested that I didn't fulfill the conditions for administering spiritual activities in public.

Václav Maly

But obviously I know very well, why. First, because I signed Charter 77. Also because I was a member of the Committee for the Defense of the Unjustly Persecuted. This made them think that I had great influence on believers, above all, on young men. These are the specific reasons why I lost the state license.

I was without a defense. Afterwards, I had to search for menial work. But not just for any menial work. It had to be isolated menial work. For example, I wanted to work in a hospital, but I was told, it isn't possible, because I might influence the patients in their beds. I wanted to work in a factory. But I couldn't, because the secret policemen didn't wish to see me among workers. Finally, I was allowed to work shovelling coal. So I became a furnace stoker in various Prague hotels for many years.

Finally, I ended up cleaning lavatories in the subway. But even then I was always followed by the secret police and I was many, many times interrogated. This new style of life wasn't easy. But in a way, this time was blessed, because I could be with the ordinary citizens. I could live their problems. And they were more open to me because they saw that I lived the same style of life they did.

For example, I had to ride the crowded trains and buses and shop in the empty stores. The people recognized that I did this from conviction, and that I had none of the privileges of my profession. Then, they opened their hearts to me. I came to recognize, really, the soul of the ordinary citizen.

When I was still in my church, I could meet only those few who already believed and chose to come. But it was different in the hotels and subways. For me, it was very important that I could connect my intellectual work with the daily life of the ordinary citizens. It was enriching.

But could you practice as a priest during that time?

Obviously it was dangerous to continue priestly activities underground. The punishment for doing so, according to a special paragraph in the law, was two years imprisonment.

I ignored this danger. I lectured. I held Bible lessons. I instructed children. I prepared people for confirmation. Performed baptisms and weddings. I had family circles and was active in the religious samizdat. I wrote articles. In fact, I would say that my public priestly life was richer precisely because of the constant danger of imprisonment.

Samizdat (Russian: self-published) *refers to the books, pamphlets, magazines and broadsides that were published in Soviet Block countries without the official permission of the state. Writing, publishing or possessing these underground publications was forbidden.*

And the connection between your own spiritual life and these political issues?

The connection is always there. As Mr. Solzhenitsyn said, when one stops a lie, even at the smallest point, something happens. Even if it isn't seen by the eyes of the world.

This is why I wasn't disappointed, for example, that for many years, Charter 77 was only a very small group, and a group even disdained by ordinary citizens of the Czechoslovakia. I was very often told it is was a vain attempt. I wasn't disappointed, because I saw it on another level.

But now God has given us concrete evidence that this position has been successful. Not only during the November events of 1989, but even before that as more and more people joined us.

If one relies only on success in life, it is very dangerous and one can be very, very often disappointed, and sorry. This life of competition sees only the goal to be successful. But it isn't—it isn't the main thing—that matters in the human life. The main thing is the possibility to sacrifice something for other men. To love other men. To be able to offer something to other men. To be able to trust. To be able to create a community which is full of mutual trust.

When you teach children in a class, what is the most important thing for them to understand about faith, religion or their choice of faith or religion?

The study of the Bible. I try to show children those stories, and let them be touched be their power. These are stories about concrete behavior of men. I try to show children that faith can be incorporated into daily life. Faith travels in the company of certain values, which can be lived at schools, at home or with friends.

Professor Hejdánek of the Church of the Czech Brethren

In general, in the context of Eastern Europe, how severely were the churches in Czechoslovakia repressed? All churches.

The repressions of the churches started in different ways. First of all, repression against the Catholic church began after 1948. The Protestant churches, which were a minority in this country, survived without massive repressions for a time. They might have represented examples of the possibility of Christians living within a socialist country.

The Catholic church, represented, and represents even now, the vast majority of religious-oriented people. It represented at the same time a dangerous element in society which could have influenced the political situation. Therefore, it was repressed massively.

Ladislav Hejdánek is a professor of Protestant theology at Charles University in Prague. The Evangelical Church of the Czech Brethren is Czechoslovakia's largest evangelical Protestant church.

What kind of repression are we talking about?

Well, very soon after February '48 within two years, monks were interned....

Imprisoned?

No, No. It was only internment in some camps or in some buildings somewhere outside of Prague and the bigger towns. And they had to work physically there in those buildings. They were isolated from the society. Priests also.

Some of the priests were imprisoned, but this also happened to laymen. Many laymen, especially people who were respected by other people and who could generate political and moral resistance.

In general how effective was this policy of massive repression? Were the churches fundamental in the process of the revolution, or was the government quite successful in general in keeping the lid on and the power away from the churches?

Well, if I have to evaluate the effectiveness of the official repression, then I'm not quite sure if I'm right, but I observe it, in a sense, as a positive factor. Because to some degree what the church did achieve during these years, and even today, would not have been possible with this repression.

I don't believe that the repression had any real result. It only showed that Christians are not so strong and spiritually and mentally in order.

We can start by looking at the Catholic church. The repressions were oriented first against the hierarchy. Clearly, much was dependent from the hierarchy. The normal people in the church, the laymen, didn't know what to do. They were perplexed by the repressions.

Consequently, during these 40 years they became much more developed. They had to act on their own initiative. They could not depend on the church hierarchy. Therefore, to that certain degree, I think the repression had a positive effect.

As for the Protestant churches, we can observe that because the Protestant churches were not so massively repressed as the Catholics, they were not as prepared for new repressions after 1968. The Catholics were much more prepared for resistance than the Protestants were. So, of course, the repression was against democracy, against human rights

Ladislav Hejdánek

and so on, but in truth it had also a positive role in the development of strength within the churches.

In this 40 years of communism, how was the behavior in general of your church?

It seems to me that in my church, the Evangelical Church of the Czech Brethren, many people were convinced, like me, that Protestants were an elite within the society. We soon found that we were not prepared for resistance.

There were many people who were generally against the regime, quite openly, but without understanding what was really going on. Their resistance, or their opposition was less effective, less intelligent, less clever than it might have been.

Could you tell me about the time that Brezhnev came to town and you and other dissidents were rounded up?

Yes. It was two years after the founding of the movement called Charter 77. Actually, it was no movement. It was only a statement that people signed saying that they were convinced that human rights are very necessary for society, and nothing more. When Brezhnev visited Prague, most of the signers of Charter 77 were imprisoned for the time Brezhnev was in town. We were all in prison for four days; each in our own cell. And during this time in Ruzyn prison, we had the marvelous opportunity to talk with one another because of the prison's marvelous acoustics. It was necessary only to speak out of the small cell windows, and everyone else could hear clearly. It was like a telephone.

We talked all day and night this way and it was impossible to stop us because there were about 200 of us. As soon as they stopped one of us, others would start up, and so on all day.

When Soviet Premier Brezhnev visited Prague in 1979, dissident Czechs were rounded up and held in Prague's Ruzyn prison for the duration of the visit. The intention of the Communist regime was to hide any signs of unrest, but the result was essentially a state-sponsored convention of dissident intellectuals.

I'd love to know about the evolution of the behavior of resistance and/or collaboration of your church?

After the takeover of the Communist in February '48, most of the members of our church proved that the criticism of professor of theology Hromádka, a very important person in the Protestant movement in this country, was right. His criticism was that our church is for the most part socially and politically oriented to accomodate the needs of a modern bourgeois society.

Of course this is a generality to a certain degree, but it was to a certain degree true. Most of these members of our church and other Protestant churches reacted as people endangered primarily on a social and economic level. They didn't behave like real Christians.

Certainly, they criticized the Communists for their social planning and the methods of their police and so on. But, for instance, they did not protest against the repression of their Catholic brothers. They did not stand solidly with all Christians in this country.

I can't understand it. Even Professor Hromádka, who criticized the church, didn't protest at this time.

When the pressure and repression was suddenly turned against them, how did the church react? How did it behave?

When the cruelest repressions against the Catholic church began, most of the Protestants simply accepted it as historical justice, because the Catholic church was responsible for many similar attacks and repressions against the Protestant churches after the Thirty Years War. But then, when the repression spread to all churches after 1968, the Catholics, because they had been repressed already for 20 years, were more prepared to resist than the Protestants were.

And what did the Protestants do? How would you characterize their behavior?

They were not prepared and many of them were so weak that they began to collaborate. Many other stopped all their political activities and political responsibility in the society. They simply concentrated on pietistically reading the Bible. And there were many people who just left the church and began acting like they were people who had never been Christians.

Of course, there were some exceptional people, but as a whole the great majority of the people, and the pastor, were profoundly perplexed. They behaved cautiously. They collaborated under pressure, without a real sense of doing something wrong.

Now the people who thought then that it was the best thing to do to collaborate and give information to the police or to some functionary of

Ladislav Hejdánek

the state, now they are not able to accept that they are co-responsible for the general state of the society. They are convinced that their individual situations were much more complicated and difficult than that of the dissidents, for instance.

Is it your view that in order to move forward, the church has to at least address the issue of its past?

Yes. I see it as a big crisis in the ability to face the future. If somebody is not able to evaluate critically the past, then he will be unable to face the important issues of the future. It's a true catastrophe. Not economically. Economics will be resolved over the next 20 years or so. But morally and spiritually, it's a catastrophe. Now is the time when Christians should go forward with their mission of helping the people to understand the situation in a moral sense. But they have nothing to do and nothing to say to others. The Christians seem not to be able to help society. And I think it's a consequence of the incapability to see their own role in the last 20 or 40 years.

Please tell me more about this moral catastrophe.

It is a moral and spiritual catastrophe, and it has several levels. During the first weeks after the so-called revolution here in Czechoslovakia nobody objected to the slogans of the students: "We want no violence, even against the police." They held to this slogan even after there was no longer any threat from the police.

No one objected then, but now people are so full of hate, not primarily against the police, but against people who collaborated, that they talk of massive investigations. It would be like examining everyone to see if they were registered with the police as collaborators. This is so full of hate, and so irrational. Who can fairly evaluate the reasons someone may have had for collaborating? Some people were coerced, for instance.

People are not able to control themselves. They don't understand that even St. Peter accommodated himself to fear, and that after Golgotha, the disciples of Jesus disappeared. They did this, and you see, they could start again. Today, nobody now is prepared to accept that the people who are registered in the police archives as informers, could start fresh again.

So what should the church do? It too is caught in the same dilemma. Should it investigate itself? Should it be quiet? Should it be generous?

I prefer to speak about Christians, individual Christians, rather than about the church. A Christian should behave in such a way that he is a good example for others.

For instance, the people who collaborated in the church should openly express themselves, and what they did. And the church could then react in a way that would be a model for others.

Who should take this initiative in a society if not the church? But it's not possible to forgive people for doing something bad if they don't openly say they did something wrong. That's the problem.

Let me now ask you about your own struggle with conscience. What was the most difficult choice for you between the dictates of your conscience and what was safe for you and your family:?

You see, I'm a philosopher. I do not frequently use religious expressions to explain things. In my view conscience is something like a reaction to challenges coming from the future. Truth is something which doesn't exist now but which is coming from the future. But we all have to answer to this truth.

In my view, all faith is simply the orientation of a human life to the coming future. The main miracle in this world is that after every second, after every minute, after every hour, comes another one. If not, this world is nothing. And so, the main thing is not to be afraid of being imprisoned, and not to see only dangers, but to have a basic hope that the right things, the true things will come from the future. We are waiting for them, but we are actively waiting. We have to go towards them, to act, so that we may help truth and justice to be realized, to be exercised, to be real.

I wonder in your own context, was there ever a time where you feared for your actions?

Well, see, I'm not quite normal. I have skin like an elephant. So that I don't feel any fear in exposed situations. But I feel fear in quiet situations, where nothing happens. I felt perhaps the worst fear after 1970 when it was not quite clear what I should do. Then I was imprisoned in 1971, and

Ladislav Hejdánek

that solved my problem. Suddenly, I was deprived of my fears because, then of course, I knew what to do.

In fact, I couldn't do anything in the prison. But I was useful just by being imprisoned. It was a sort of a protest for me, and I must say that I was much more free imprisoned than I was before I was arrested.

But I don't think this is a normal reaction. I was terribly depressed before I went to prison, and then I found my way. After being released, I was already oriented through my imprisonment. So I don't think that conscience is something contradictory to fear. It seems to me that fear can be a result of having conscience. Because we understand that we should be doing something new and we don't know what. It is conscience that is depressing us.

Now, nobody is very happy if he has to decide about himself, about his family and so on, you see? It's very difficult to start with provoking activities or protests against the opposition if you know that you have four children, as I have four small children.

But if the other side starts with repression, and imprisonment, then it's solved. I could not do anything else. I do it for the society, and for my children. Thus I find my way.

Father Kansky: The Borders of Fear and Conscience

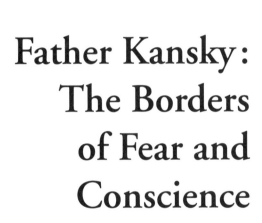

In the context of other countries in Eastern Europe over the past 40 years, could you help out my audience that doesn't know anything about the issues of church and state? Where are the churches repressed by the Communist governments? And how does the repression in Czechoslovakia compare with other countries?

The situation of the church in Europe, in this part of Europe, which was occupied and under the influence of the Soviet Union, was different, because in Poland Catholicism was part of the national character. What the Poles wanted, the church wanted as well.

In Czechoslovakia, the situation was totally different. Historically,

Alois Kansky, a young Czech Catholic priest, arranged for the funeral service of Jaroslav Seifert in 1986. Seifert, who had been awarded the Nobel Prize for Literature in 1984, had helped to found the Czechoslovak Communist Party in the '20s. His avant-garde activities and supposed bourgeois sentiments provoked his expulsion from the party in 1929. He signed Charter77 shortly before his death.

29

from the time of the Hussites and from the creation of the Czechoslovak Republic in 1918, there were always pressures against Catholicism. And the Communists, in 1948, were able to work with it, and they succeeded.

With two things they succeeded: first of all, they succeeded in isolating the normal person from religion as such, but the most important thing was that different churches were isolated from each other as well–Catholics, Evangelics and the Czechoslovak Hussite Church. Contacts between them were possible only under the supervision of the state and the Communist officials. And what the Communists could afford to do in Czechoslovakia, like locking up the priests and believers, could never happen in Poland.

So, to make it simpler, in Czechoslovakia, there was never any law which would forbid religious activities or churches. But, in fact, it was already reduced to an official cult, which is not the same as the freedom of religion.

Explain the phrase "official cult."

When I say the official cult, I am talking about what actually was happening in the church. Marriages and such. But this was happening under the supervision of the state.

How did the state actually manage to control? I mean, this whole idea of licensing priests is completely foreign to an American.

It was very simple. If I wanted to be a priest, officials in the Ministry of Culture had to allow me to go to the seminary to study. After finishing and being ordained to be a priest, the state decided if I could go on and work as a priest. They could give me permission, or not to give me permission. This is one thing.

The second thing is that everything that happened in this realm had to be under the control of the special secretary for churches at the National Committee or Ministry of Culture.

And what punishments did the state have at its disposal?

If somebody was guilty against the so-called "state supervision of the church," if he did something extraordinary or something different, if he was a priest, this government approval was taken away from him, and he

Alois Kansky

had to wash windows. This happened to the new Prague Archbishop Metislav Vlk.

The second sanction concerned the believers. They could have some problems in their work. And the last thing would be that a person would be judged for acting differently and convicted. For example, believers were stripped and beaten. These things happened frequently. So fear always hung over the religious life, especially over the church.

What were some of your own problems in trying to balance between your conscience and having your state license revoked?

You know, to speak about the development of your own conscience, bravery and vice versa is very difficult, because the human being is really ashamed after being afraid. Maybe the first time in my life I was really afraid was when after three weeks I returned from the seminary, and the state police appeared at my flat. I was nineteen years old. They let me know that they could call me anytime, and that they could do whatever they wanted.

It was something else to be in the seminary, to be a student where nothing was happening, something else from being a priest. In Pilsen, for example, where I was working with Václav Maly, they invited me to some discussion, and this state police officer said to me "My name is Václav Havel." I realized then that they could do anything.

Václav Maly signed the petition which became very famous in our country, Charter 77. It was a civic activity against the totalitarian regime. And its head was Václav Havel. Today he's President of Czechoslovakia. I asked myself then how my friend Maly could dare to sign the charter. He also became a member of the Committee for the Unjustly Persecuted.

He was beaten up, and permissions were taken away from him, and finally he was put to jail without any trial for three-quarters of a year. And I was asking myself, how is it possible that he can do it and I can't? And the answer is very simple. I was afraid. I was afraid that what he went through I wouldn't be able to go through. I was afraid that they would just hit me over the face and I would crack. And then I would be embarrassed. I would be ashamed of myself.

For me the border of the fear was at the point of collaboration with the Communists. I knew that I couldn't become a member of Pacem In Terris, which was the organization of the priests who were loyal to the

Appointed to follow Frantisek Tomasek as Cardinal in 1990, Metislav Vlk, Bishop of Ceské Budejovice, had worked for years in the underground church after having his license to practice as a priest suspended.

Communist regime. For him, this border was somewhere else. He had to sign the Charter 77.

He's a typical example of the person who, although he was suffering much, never held anything against anybody who didn't dare to go to the same way he went. But I wasn't like Václav. I wasn't able to kick the police out of my apartment. I was willing to speak to them. He wasn't willing to speak to them. He just kicked them out.

What was the most difficult period in this decision to stick by what your conscience had told you?

These are difficult moments, when a human being is on the border between fear and heroism. Every person has plenty of these moments in his or her life. I became well-known during the Communist times because the family of the famous Czech poet, Jaroslav Seifert, the only laureate of the Nobel Prize for literature in our country, asked me to arrange a funeral for him. What happened to me before the funeral of Seifert, those eleven days, were probably the most difficult days in my whole life.

I was thinking whether it was worse than when my mother was dying from cancer and I was only twenty-one years old. At the time before the funeral, I had the same feelings of helplessness, anger, fear. But at the same time, there was something of a longing to do exactly this thing. Like to be with my mother in the worst moments, or to prepare this funeral for this man, who was known by the whole nation. And for me this ceremony was the greatest honor I received in my life.

First of all, why were the Communists worried about your giving a funeral mass for Seifert? What did he represent to them? What were you put through?

What were they afraid of? They were afraid that the funeral for the Jaroslav Seifert, who received the Nobel Prize, but also who signed the Charter 77, would become some kind of a national, or maybe even a religious manifestation.

The second thing that they were afraid of was that this funeral would give exposure to the most honest people, like Václav Havel. And this is why they didn't want me to do it.

His family met me first during my service. It was fourteen days

Alois Kansky

before the funeral. The police were really trying to arrange it so that it would be taken care of by a priest from Pacem In Terris, who would just speak boringly in cliches. The state was afraid of a spontaneous reaction from the nation, and this was such a good moment for it. So they were trying to do everything possible to prevent it from becoming an expression of support for religion and justice.

What was going on inside of you? That's what I want to get at.

It was January of 1986. I was thirty-one years old at that time. Against me weren't just officials, but the whole computer center. I was even invited to the Ministry of Culture, and before the beginning of the service, Mr. Jelinek asked me if we had permission to bury Mr. Seifert, since he was in the Communist Party. And I had to explain to this official that Mr. Seifert left the Communist Party in 1929. We were even afraid that if I went to this Ministry, they could put me in jail, and then bring in another priest. But this didn't happen.

In arranging this funeral, I realized a very essential thing. I, who never did anything heroic in my life, had to stand next to the grave of this person who did everything for this nation and did everything possible for justice. For that reason he signed the Charter 77, and for that reason he received the Nobel Prize for Literature.

And at that point, a tough, and very essential fight was born inside of me. Do I have to do what the officials are asking me to do? Prepare an unsalty, boring final parting for Seifert? Or should I stand on the side of the people who have been persecuted and make of this funeral a spontaneous manifestation of trust, faith, justice, and truth.

In the end I decided that I wasn't going to be intimidated and that I was going to do it the way I felt it should be and the way this person deserved.

And the consequences?

The results of such a funeral could have been anything. The authorities could have revoked my state permit, maybe put me in jail, but my biggest fear was really that maybe at night they would come to the church and just beat me up, or maybe not even to the church, but that they would just catch me at some corner and beat me up. I hate to admit it, but I was afraid of the physical pain. Maybe because my heart is not as good as it should be. I was afraid of pain.

The actual funeral was little bit like a dream after this eleven days of constant problems with the state officials and police. It was a relief, a liberation. One of the basic feelings I had was that I just wanted to be done with it. Five or seven thousand people were there, I can't even say how many. They allowed us to put loud speakers in front of the church. I received this permission at 10:30 P.M. one day before the funeral. Unbelievable. One of our best opera singer, Josef Kamer, sang. One of the best actors, Ota Sklencka, spoke. The best of the nation was there. This very event became much more important than just a funeral for one person. It became the demonstration of national feeling. And this was 1986, four years before the revolution.

Do you think that certain people like Popieluszko, Havel, Maly, seem to not have this fear that so many of us share? They seem to swim upstream so effortlessly. What is that quality? Is it genetic?

No. To heroically overcome fear has much deeper roots, but it is much more simple than genetics. For example, I might be involved in something that I know might end up badly. I will search for a compromise and look for some solution. People like Václav Maly and Václav Havel, or Father Popieluszko simply do not allow themselves to have any internal conversation with evil. They will have no discussion with the forces of violence. But me? I would try to discuss it.

What do you think is the appropriate guideline between politics and the affairs of conscience? How do you draw the line as a priest, between what is appropriate and inappropriate action, just for yourself?

A priest shouldn't really get mixed up with politics, but let's understand it correctly. A human being by nature is political. I can not be elected to the Parliament, or anywhere else. I can't be engaged politically in this way. But Václav Maly understood that it was a question of justice. And he felt it when he had to sign Charter 77, or to be part of the Committee for the Unjustly Persecuted. It has nothing to do with politics, it's just defending truth and justice. And he said correctly that the priests should be on the front line of this fight.

Alois Kansky

But members of the opposition really weren't that safe in the church here because the church was so carefully controlled. It seemed to burst out into theaters. Am I wrong about that?

Look, I could tell about many meetings which happened in the Church of Brevnov, where I worked for five years. If the police knew about them, or didn't know, I have no idea. But the issue is that I didn't sign Charter 77, and I didn't do anything against the regime actively. I didn't fight against the establishment actively.

What I said in church was one thing, but if I had one private Mass or two private Masses in a private flat, I would be more persecuted than if I preached openly against the government in church. What they were afraid of was conspiracy, that something was happening behind their backs.

If you look at the church's behavior over the last 20 years, up until '89, was it a firm source of resistance to Communist authority?

To compare churches, and ask which one was more involved in the fight against communism, is nonsense. I can say that in the Catholic church, there were decent people who took part in the resistance. The same thing was true of the Evangelics. But as a whole, no church or religious community could receive an A grade.

Each church had some kind of a center of gravity, like Cardinal Tomasek or Maly, or Alfred Kocáb in the Evangelical church, for example.

As a whole, the church was the only institution that during this long miserable period was persistent in its belief in democracy and truth. Of course, we understand that there were some people who failed in different ways, but, as a whole, the church was alone as an institution that believers could look up to.

This explains the strange post-November 1989 disappointment when people realized that the representatives of the church, the priests, were speaking the same way they spoke during the Communist years. They didn't show joy and euphoria over the fact that they could now openly tell people what is the truth.

Is it true that for the Catholic church to move forward it would help to look back and see how well it did in the face of communism?

Certainly it would be very good if the Catholic church in our country would be willing to look back at the last 40 years of its past. But I can't tell you openly who should do it. Bishops? Those we have now, they are not going to do it. Some of them are from the old guard, from the old times, and they could be successfully attacked for this life they led.

Who can evaluate all this? I personally think that it should just be left alone. We should wait for the future historians, who wouldn't be burdened by the past and who would be able to express freely what really happened.

Briefly, who was Mr. Jelinek and what was he doing?

Well, Mr. Jelinek was a director of the Secretariat for the church in the Ministry of Culture of the Czech Socialist Republic. He had underneath him many workers whose only duty was to make it as difficult as possible for the church, although they said otherwise.

What did Mr. Jelinek do to you?

Mr. Jelinek didn't do anything wrong to me. Except that two hours before Seifert's funeral I had to come to his office. He decided who is going to have state permission, which church is going to receive what amount of money, and so on. He was a typical representative of the Communist totalitarian power.

What did he say to you when you saw him?

Two hours before the Seifert funeral, I went to his office and he told me, "Of course you realize that this funeral can uplift you to the skies, or"— and I don't think I want to tell you what he said next.

Okay. Forgive a real newsman's question. Did you see the events of '89 coming? Did you have any idea that this power would be swept away so fast? And what was your involvement in those days of November and December?

The weakening of the Communist regime could be felt in 1985 and 1986. In 1988 and early in 1989, people went abroad who could never go abroad before, so clearly something was happening. My role in all this

Alois Kansky

was quite small. I was invited to the National Theater and the National Opera House, and then at St. Markéta Church in Brevnov we arranged a prayer meeting of all the churches which existed in Prague at that time. It became very famous.

You see, the basic feeling I had at the beginning of the November Revolution was incredible anger. Maybe for the first time in my life I felt something like hatred when I realized that helpless children were being beaten up on the national avenue.

I wasn't sure if they were going to send tanks to Prague, or if they were going to send jets to Letná Stadium and just kill everybody there. All I felt was fear and anger. Later came euphoria, but it came only after the election of the President.

How do you feel about your own church? What is your relationship to it?

You know, if I have to be totally open and honest, I will tell you that I'm living through a lot of grief and sadness, because I think the church and a lot of the servants of the church have forgotten the message they have to carry. What is happening in the church is happening in the whole society. People do not know what to do with this sudden freedom.
People talk about the return of property, houses and fields. And travelling abroad, and going to college and how things need to be renovated. There is nothing to renovate here. We have to create totally new things. Everything is destroyed and devastated. Moral qualities are devastated. A whole generation is uneducated.

A lot of us are trying to do what is really important. Schools for the children. Hope for the future. But it seems we are just falling to this thing, this thing that you in America have fallen to for such a long time, this material thing. We are putting material things above everything, as if it were not so important that, for example, I love you.

Is there anything you would like to talk about briefly that I haven't brought up with you today?

If you are making a film about the borders between heroism and cowardice, I think that you have chosen very good place, Central Europe. You should show to your American viewers what it is to be afraid, to be really scared of expressing your own beliefs.

And mainly, you should not judge. You shouldn't judge people for what they have done from fear, because you don't know anything about it, you didn't live through this.

Mr. Jelinek of the Ministry of Culture

Could you tell me what your job was in the government? And please describe the purpose of your ministry.

I have worked as a director of the secretariat for religious matters at the Ministry of Culture in the Government of the Czech Socialist Republic since 1974. This section was one of the divisions at the Ministry of Culture, actually directed under the Minister of Culture.

And what was its purpose?

I would say that our obligation and function was to fulfill the statute that was there to adjust the mutual relations between the Czech Republic and the church and other religious organizations.

It was the task of the Ministry of Culture to monitor the activities of the churches in Czechoslovakia. As such, the Ministry had power over the licensing of priests and pastors. Mr. Jelinek was the director of the the Ministry's secretariat for religious matters from 1974 to 1989.

And what was the object of this statute? Was it to help the churches become bigger and better, or was it to help them to be smaller and more obedient?

I want to say that my function, as well as the function of other local departments, was to fulfill the prescribed law that was accepted in 1949. It deals with the state economic security and its relation to the churches. It means that the church has the right to turn to the state authorities and request economic help. The state then supplied whatever was necessary for the cult's existence and for what was needed for repairs.

This role was, of course, much broader. The additional duties of the authorities of state management was not-and I say this quite openly-only to see if these laws-valid laws- were being obeyed, but also to protect the churches in situations when other authorities and institutions might somehow break those laws.

What might a minister or a priest or a pastor do that could be viewed by you and your ministry as a problem. I am not talking about money now. What would be something that they might say or do or preach that would be upsetting to you as the minister in charge of controlling the church?

As I have already said, there was the possibility of a regular communication and contact with church representatives and individual priests. And that was applicable at all levels of the department. We had the opportunity to discuss any questions at any time. They also had the chance to turn to us when they needed.

Employees of the local national committee in charge of these matters would be, for example, invited to higher church meetings so they could observe and obtain information about the problems of the church that would be of interest from a state point of view. In fact, there were even friendly encounters between the authorities from the state administration and the representatives of the church and the religious organizations. Contact between us was on an almost daily basis, if you understand what I am saying.

Could you give me a concrete example of what a priest or a pastor might do or say that would attract your attention and call for correction?

Frantisek Jelinek

It sometimes might happen that certain confrontations arose during these meetings. It was not always possible to comply with all the the requests of each party. I think the most strenuous situations developed in the cases of granting state licenses. These were situations in which the church representatives, according to law, needed to obtain certain decisions for the state authorities.

The license for a bishop was handled at the highest level of government, whereas licenses for parish priests were granted by local boards. It happened in certain cases on all levels that the application to perform religious services was rejected for a particular priest.

Could you give me an example of something a particular priest of minister or bishop might do that would upset you and cause you to take such action?

The law would have to be broken. It could have been all kinds of things. At this moment I cannot think of a typical example that would explain this whole problem. It could have been some criminal activity-from the point of view of the law or some behavior that stepped out of the frame of a given law that was supposed to be obeyed by the whole of society.

Well, if a priest or pastor urged someone to speak up for their human rights or to speak out against the government for any reason, would that have been a problem for your ministry?

Not for our ministry. Under no circumstances. As far as these matters were concerned, to speak about human rights or about Christian obligations toward one's own church, that was an entirely common matter.

But perhaps you are thinking about a question dealing with certain separate political views that differed from the official ideology. Someone could, for example, be a member of a certain group that, I would say, acted differently-inconsistently-with our law. I know of such cases. But this would be under the jurisdiction of the local committees. We have negotiated these matters with bishops. These discussions were quite open. We would agree on certain matters.

Sometimes we would not share the same opinions. But there were always certain principles that we had to follow and there were certain borders for the churches.

Which church in your experience in the last ten or 15 years was the best behaved and which was the biggest problem?

It is difficult to say. The truth is that the Roman Catholic church had the most members and the major standing. If you permit me, I would like to use a certain quote of Cardinal Tomasek who was interviewed recently the Czechoslovak magazine *Kvety*. With your permission, I would like to read this quotation. And after that I would like to add my opinion. Will you give me permission? I have it here just by chance, because I was just reading it. I respect the Cardinal tremendously because he is a very honest and fair human being. I will, if you permit me, read this quote from the interview and then, afterwards, I would like to present my opinion. Is that possible?

Please, just tell me about it in brief now and you can read it later on.

Okay. I have the article with me. I marked it because it is very interesting and I wouldn't like to distort the picture of its context. Could I please read it word by word to you. It is very interesting. Mr. Cardinal says in this interview that *(reads)* "if necessary, Catholics together with the church are obligated to intervene in the situations that do not comply with the basic character of the Christian view. Regardless of the social level at which the situation occurs."

I think this is the point of that interview. Mr. Cardinal is reacting to the question of what position the church took in the political evolution prior to the "velvet revolution." He was asked if the church perhaps politicized too much in the area of politics here. And Mr. Cardinal answered that it is the duty of the church and every Christian to take a stand against certain principles of political evolution. Not only here, but everywhere.

And would you describe Cardinal Tomasek as being helpful to your government? And if so, can you give me an example of how he was helpful?

I quoted Cardinal Tomasek purposely, first of all, because I have known him for the last 25 years. We talked very often about current developments and about political matters. And about the role of the church. The

Frantisek Jelinek

Cardinal talks about moral principles, principles of a Christian that had, according to him, been broken. That's when he felt that it was his duty to express his opinion.

Cardinal Tomasek was an elder statesman of the church. But Vaclav Maly was someone who was very much involved in the opposition to the government. Was he, for instance, a problem at all for your ministry? What did you think of Vaclav Maly, who was so active in the opposition? What did Cardinal Tomasek think of him?

As for Václav Maly, the Roman Catholic priest, he did not cause us any personal problems. He was one of the Charter 77 members and was very involved there. I had the opportunity to personally discuss this fact with Cardinal Tomasek.

It was because Mr. Maly, a priest, was involved with Charter 77 that he did not receive a state license. When we discussed the issues, we concluded that Mr. Maly, a priest, became, as one of the signers of Charter 77, someone who worked in opposition to the official ideology, the official politics, and that was the real reason for his leaving the church. He himself chose this political route. He did not leave the church because he was suspended by Cardinal Tomasek, he left because he did not share the same political ideas of the state.

But what did he do wrong?

Mr. Václav Maly was a Catholic priest. Personally, I think he was not a bad person, but he was of a different political conviction. He chose the road of political opposition. And because of that reason, he lost his license in his district. Those authorities accountable for assigning or terminating licenses-so you will understand-punished him by removing his state license to practice as a priest. I don't know him personally. I never had the opportunity. Mr. Maly worked presumably outside the church before returning back to his function.

As for my conversation with Cardinal Tomasek about Mr. Maly, the priest, we did not have entirely the same opinion in this matter, because the Cardinal saw no reason to punish Mr. Maly for not sharing the same political convictions. The situation was a bit complicated by the fact that, as far as the state authorities were concerned, he was a priest who broke the law- or the rule.

And what do you personally think should have happened to him? Should he have been imprisoned?

Jail in no case. It was a personal decision. It is difficult to punish somebody for his political opinions, his beliefs, or his conscience. It is a personal thing.

But Father Maly and other priests who expressed their opinion were in prison. He was beaten at least on one occasion. Do you think that was going too far?

I don't think there was any reason for imprisonment. He was sufficiently punished by the fact that he was not able to practice his religious duties. It is not easy for a priest to lose his profession.

The poet Jaroslav Seifert, the Nobel laureate, when his funeral was announced, was that a problem for you? And was the priest involved in that ever talked to by you?

There was no problem from our side. As far as I know the mass was conducted without any problems. At least from the point of view of the church.

Father Kansky, the priest involved, told me that he was really quite terrified by his decision to go ahead with the mass, because the government wanted to stop him. You, in particular, wanted it stopped. Do you remember any of that?

In what sense?

Well, in the sense that the government-your ministry-wanted him not to hold the mass for Seifert, who had signed Charter 77 and was generally in opposition to the government.

But the funeral took place.

But I was told that it took place despite the urgent desire of the government to stop it.

Frantisek Jelinek

I did not understand. That they wanted to stop it, or did not want to stop it? You mean coordinate it?

Let me ask again. Father Kansky told me that your ministry, or your office, or you personally wanted that mass not to be held, because Seifert, although he was a famous poet, was in opposition to the government. And so the government did not want an enormous service to honor him.

If I remember well, the Ministry of Culture did not issue an order to stop the mass for Mr. Seifert in the church where Mr. Kansky practiced his religion.

And did you ever talk, yourself, to Father Kansky, or did anybody that you know of, talk to him and ask him to stop the funeral.

I? I have not talked to him about these matters. Maybe this needs to be clarified. Who from the Ministry of Culture was supposed to have to talk to him about this? Maybe it could have been someone from another division whose responsibility it was. But as for the order to stop the service for Mr. Seifert, it did not come from our office.

You have talked about the borders of behavior that you discussed with Cardinal Tomasek. Can you give me a kind of condensed example of what these boundaries were?

There were many discussions with Cardinal Tomasek. About many matters. One example-in my opinion a very important one-concerned issues of religious organizations. Some congregations and orders were disqualified in this country in the '50s. We knew it was necessary to deal with this problem. Especially with the case of women's orders.

During our talks we managed to come to certain conclusions. We made it possible for novices to enter into individual orders and congregations in our country. These discussions were not uncomplicated since there were certain obstructions from the law. We had to search for the optimal results. So women who were seriously interested in working in individual congregations could enter these orders. We concluded that the state shall not decline the admission of women to Czech congregations through the Czech Catholic charity.

Mr. Jelinek, are you yourself a believer? Were you ever christened or were you brought up as a member of any faith?

I consider myself an atheist, even though I was brought up and was confirmed in the Czech Evangelic church, and-to be honest-I must say that I have very nice memories of those times. The priest whom I knew then, when I was still a young boy, a very long time ago, was a very kind and friendly man. I have very nice memories of him. I even met his son, who is also a priest, in Prague. Very nice people.

Did that church, the Czech Evangelic Brethren cause a lot of problems for your ministry?

One cannot say if their behavior was good or bad. There were certain problems. Same as in other churches. Some priests had different opinions than others. The expressed their political views, like Mr. Maly.

We had a situation, in 1987 or '88 or '89, when several priests signed a document. And because of that, the local national authorities revoked their licenses. The Ministry of Culture, our department, cancelled this decision and the priests were allowed to continue their duties.

Do you yourself, personally, think it was right to punish someone for expressing a religious belief that is not in conformity with the state? How do you feel about that, looking back?

In my opinion each man has the right to believe in whatever he wants. And to try to change conscience or faith by applying authority is absurd. I could be an atheist. Someone else might be a Catholic or an Evangelical, but that is a personal affair. Of course, even if he is a priest or a preacher, he must observe certain religious laws. But everyone has a free alternative.

But priests weren't just under the law of the church. He was licensed by your office, which was generally known to be one of the strictest and toughest in Europe.

Could I ask you something first? Do you mean to say that our office was the toughest? Should I understand the question that way?

Your government was among the harshest in Eastern Europe.

Frantisek Jelinek

I would like to understand your question. When you talk about the government do you mean the state as such, or the department that handles these matters. Because we did not punish anybody. We did not judge anybody through the section that dealt with religious matters.

I mean the government which you served. Both your ministry and whatever police agency watched the church.

You mean the state as the whole, as the government authority. If you mean the Ministry of Justice, or the courts, these were matters not connected with us. We had nothing to do with these problems.

Did you have the power to remove a priest's license?

Our office that handled these matters did not have this power. The appropriate local state authorities had the right to do so.

Were they not under your control?

These organs had full authority and made their own decisions.

In your opinion, after years and years in government, watching the church, was your mission successful? Did the state control the church? Or did any church play a role in the revolution of 1989? Was the church strong enough to help the revolution that overthrew your government in 1989?

Could you possibly repeat that question, please?

Did the church have a significant role in the revolution of 1989? Do you understand?

Do you mean did our department influence talks with the church at the time of the revolution?

Was any church strong enough to help the revolution which overthrew your government in 1989?

Do you mean the government as a whole, or as a state government authority? I have already talked about the fact that certain churches voiced their opinions towards the political evolution at that time. On purpose I have quoted Cardinal Tomasek. The Catholic church, as the Cardinal explained, is obliged to enter and talk about these matters. And that is why Cardinal Tomasek and other priests personally commented on these matters. They were part of this process. They criticized political opinions that did not correspond with basic Christian principles. They became part of it all.

Mr. Jelinek, I would like to ask one more time did any church in Czechoslovakia play a role in the revolution which overthrew your government in 1989?

If I understand correctly, you mean decisive role, or what role?

Any significant role.

I don't understand you well.

Did any church in Czechoslovakia play a role in the revolution that overthrew your government in 1989?

I would say that the churches became part of the whole process of the revolution. To look for the exact size of the part would be difficult. But each church contributed to this process. Maybe the largest part was played by the Roman Catholic church, as the largest of all churches. Even the personal opinion of Cardinal Tomasek played a significant role.

Which statement?

I don't understand.

Which statement of Cardinal Tomasek was helpful?

As I have said, when he, as a Christian, pointed out certain things that were not that good in the society. He discussed them openly. He spoke to the nation, to those who believed in these matters. So somewhere here, he participated in the process. He spoke about justice, about morals,

Frantisek Jelinek

about certain links between mankind.

What are you doing now? What is your work now? Are you enjoying yourself? It's quite a change, I would think.

It is a significant change for me, yes. At my new job I feel basically good. Of course, each change brings a new environment. At this moment I work in a trade business. And I am satisfied. I have a chance to meet people and I think that every job that one does is important and good.

A what is your new job?

I did not understand.

What is the name of your new job?

How could I describe it? Please give me some more time. I want to describe it precisely. If I say that we offer refreshments to the public, will you be able to understand that?

What do you sell? What service do you provide?

It is a refreshment service for citizens who request it. We sell an assortment of sweets, drinks and similar goods of this sort, and I can say that I am satisfied with this work.

Did you understand? Was it clear?

The Cardinal and the Collapse of Atheism

What did the Communists have to fear about the church, the faith? What were they afraid of?

The church was not a political party, but a living organism. They knew the struggle with the church would be hard. And it was. They knew that the church and the believers would resist the terror of atheism and of the police. This was especially true in Slovakia, but it was also true in Moravia and Bohemia. It was so powerful that the regime had to collapse.

They knew what it was like to clash with Christians. They knew the Christians were not just any political party that could be dispersed without a trace. Christianity is more than just an organization. It is a matter of life and death. Believers are connected much deeper with the church than any other members of any other civic organization. The

Jan Korec was appointed by Pope John Paul II to the College of Cardinals in 1991 at the age of 67. Forty years earlier he was consecrated Bishop of Nitra in a clandestine ceremony. Between these two events he has been imprisoned several times, once for 9 years, and has worked in factories and as an elevator repairman. He has published 60 books on theological subjects.

Communists knew that. That's why they concentrated so intently of destroying the church.

They feared the church. They had the experience of struggling with the church in Russia since 1917. Their solution was to eliminate the church but not the outward organization of the church. The church, of course, is not an organization. It's an organism whose believers bring with them God, Jesus Christ resurrected.

What happened during the nights of April 13th and 14th, 1950, and explain why it happened?

It was a barbaric night. In one night, April 13th, the Communists abolished all religious orders in Czechoslovakia. The Franciscans, Dominicans, Jesuits, orders that have existed since the 11th-century convents and monasteries were erased from Bohemia, Moravia and Slovakia.

I was in Trnava that night. About 80 militiamen stormed the home of the Jesuits. They woke us up and gave us 20 minutes to pack our things and leave. There were buses waiting outside. They drove us eastwards. We thought we were being taken to Russia, but we ended up in a so-called concentration camp monastery in Slovakia. It was the Night of the Barbarians.

Where did you go after that?

Theologians and the younger people were forced into the army. Priests were gradually sent to Moravia–doctors of philosophy, theology, science–were forced to work in the fields and woods for ten years. There were no trials. Some people were later selected for trial and were sentenced to prison for ten or 15 years.

When were you sent to prison for the first time and why?

In 1960, I was sent to prison for 12 years because of my connections with the enemies of the state–those with connections with the Vatican and the young seminarians. Also because of the clandestine ordination of priests. We were considered criminals. It was said that we were more dangerous than murderers. It was an ideological struggle. An attempt at total atheization. Also the conditions in the prison were very bad.

Jan Cardinal Korec

What were these officials trying to accomplish?

They wanted to create a nation of atheists. They wanted to uproot all that was Christian. But they miscalculated. Christianity has been in our country for a thousand years–particularly in Slovakia. The first church was consecrated here in Nitra by an archbishop from Salzburg in 1129. The Communists wanted to extract all this. Our whole tradition, our national songs, schools, universities were all Christian. Christianity was inside the people. It could not be broken.

The Communists managed to do only one thing. To shove a ball under the water. But it could not be held down. It floated back up. Religion is for man so natural, it will always surface. Life is not bread alone. We had enough bread, but this was not enough. We had lost our freedom and we had stopped being human. Their intent was to turn us into a herd that would go where it was told.

But here they could see that a man is a man, not an animal–that a man needs bread, culture, freedom. He needs his conscience to be respected, and his creations to be respected. Man needs to remain man. One cannot live in a totally atheistic society. This is what our young people shouted to the world.

In all the 40 years of being in and out of prison, and under constant surveillance, did you ever lose hope that the system would change?

I was called 30 times before the secret police. But I can't say this mattered much to me. It wasn't pleasant, but it was always clear to me that I would not back down. They were waiting for that. Maybe after 17 times I would yield. But I said, "Look, you are wasting your time. It will never happen. It would mean deceiving myself. My life would be pointless."

Once I said to the interrogator–he was about my age– "You have power over me. I cannot fight with you. But understand this: I might be released and then run over by a street car. Then you shall have no more power over me. I will be where we are all going." He just looked at me.

This is where atheism collapsed. The police, all the weapons, the whole matter of physical power. People told themselves that they didn't need to become engineers. They could just be workers and they would have a better chance of remaining human. I told one officer, "You can think that I am a poor wretch. You have ordered me here. I will not fight with you. But I can think what I want. I can say what I want and do what

I want. You were ordered by your boss this morning to go out and catch Korec. That's why I do not envy you."

He looked at me, and whispered, "I don't envy myself either."

What were the conditions like in prison?

I was sentenced to prison for 12 years for my connections with the Vatican and my work with young seminarians who wanted to become priests. I met 200 other priests and five bishops in jail, and countless believers. Others came and went from jail, but we stayed.

The conditions were terrible. The work was very hard. We had to produce crystals for lamps. The production quotas were very tough and if we did not fulfill them, we would be sent to an underground correction cell for ten days. There we would sleep on wooden boards and be fed every three days. Then we would be returned to work, and if we again failed to meet the quotas we would be sent back to the correction cell.

I met one priest there, a Salezian, who had spent 80 days in the correction cell because he could not meet the quotas set for him.

There was no distinction between criminal and political prisoners. I was in one place with 13 other prisoners, 11 of whom were murderers. We were told we were worse than the murderers because we "killed" people by teaching them religion and making them dull. We were allowed to write a letter once a month, and have visitors four times a year. I spent time in a solitary cell where I learned what real tyranny is.

There were some Catholic and Evangelical priests there. Some German generals. And there were also some of the government ministers that were responsible for us being in prison. They had been jailed too.

For example, several monasteries were destroyed by the order of a Mr. Hordos. I was for ten years in relative freedom, but he was put in jail one year after he had ordered them destroyed. Life was totally insecure.

First we were enemies as believers and then someone said that this government minister is an enemy and he had to go to jail. He was beaten terribly. They said that he wanted to destroy the party from within and that he had some connections with General Tito. There was no help. There was trial after trial. It was total chaos.

A system was taking power that didn't believe in God, or in justice. Some boys in the prison told me that they were in jail for stealing. They said that when they came to trial they had told the judge, "Why are you putting us in jail? It was you who taught us that there is no God, no

Jan Cardinal Korec

heaven, no hell. And that there is no conscience." Two generations of people were brought up without a conscience and without a God.

Without God, without conscience, human life does not exist. When someone says that we are only well-developed apes, he can then talk about only two rules of morality. The fight for life and the rule of the survivor. That was Hitler's idea. That is not human morality. Human morals cannot develop from an atheistic, materialistic evolution. Only if eternity, consciousness, and God are there can man speak about a moral life.

For 20 years I have worked as a simple worker in a chemical factory. When I was 57, I began to repair elevators in Bratislava. This last year I was appointed Cardinal. In the underground church, I have written and published some 60 books. Some in Canada and in Austria, but I had no occasion to work publicly. Now I must. Even on television.

Can you give us an idea of your schedule?

From early morning, visitors are announced from all over. Then I must take care of the mail. Different organizations contact me. I was in Washington, Canada, in Rome twice. These are duties I cannot neglect. When I was consecrated bishop of Nitra, the oldest diocese in eastern and central Europe, I was 27. Now I am 67. And I am tired.

What did you say to the three policemen that tried to get you into a car just a little while ago?

There were five of them in three cars and they wanted to pull me in. Something in me protested. My father worked for 50 years in a factory. It was something of the worker's nature. I was strong and I knew that they wouldn't be able to put me in that car. After they tried and failed, they told me that I could not go home. They had strict orders not to let me go. But I told them that what I would do was my business, but they had only one thing they could do: go away.

What was your life like after you were released from prison? What has it been like for the last 15 or 20 years?

In 1969 I was treated for tuberculosis and was cured. Then I went to Rome to see Pope Paul the 6th. He had given me many gifts: a ring, a cane, and other things. Then, with the help of the Soviet Army, the period of normalization began. I couldn't work publicly as a pastor because I couldn't get a state license. The person in charge was an atheist. They even revoked my permit to work with my sisters in the hospital. So I returned to work in the chemical factory. It was hard work. I worked outside with barrels of oil and gasoline. Then I became an elevator repairman.

But I also worked in the underground church. I worked with priests, students, attorneys. I had many visitors in my room in Petrzalka. In 20 years I think I had 60,000 visitors. Many were laymen.

This was the best thing I have done. To set in motion so many people, particularly the students. They began to issue samizdats. Not even the police were able to control it.

The police knew what was going on-what we were spreading. They watched and listened to us. They interrogated us. They did not realize that the young people had no fear. This is what came from the '60s.

This is what Christianity is all about. We don't just live by ourselves. We are connected with the Holy Spirit. It unites us in one power, making us feel like brothers and sisters. Even now we feel that God's spirit is talking to us. We have difficulties, but we have hope. It is a Christian hope.

What did this room in Bratislava represent to you?

This room was my everything. My little room where I lived for 20 years. I subletted it. I ate here. Slept here and received my visitors here. It was my workplace. I wrote my manuscripts here. And I prayed here. I also performed services here, because I wasn't able to go to the church. Sometimes the young people would go to the mountains. I would go too, and meet them. I had to be careful because I was watched by the police. But my little room was my castle. Of course it was a closely watched castle. But it was home.

Why was it necessary to make you a bishop secretly?

I was consecrated bishop in 1951. After the elimination of religious orders and all seminaries, all the bishops went to prison. So there was almost no access to bishops. Still we had 500 seminarians. So once we got

Jan Cardinal Korec

to one bishop and he made priests of us, so the church could live. Then one of us was picked to be his follower as bishop. So at 27, I became the Bishop of Nitra, simply because all the other bishops had been destroyed.

Around us we created the underground church. Priests who just stayed in their offices had no chance to meet with young people. We didn't ask for permits. Today there are about 200 priests who became priests illegally without permits. Today they work legally.

What can people who have never had their faith outlawed learn from your experience?

I can say only one thing. We have survived a horrendous experience in this country, and we have realized what it means when the public life is taken over by atheists.

A boy or a girl who believed in God couldn't become a teacher. A person who believed in God couldn't go to military school or hold a public office. A believer couldn't study psychology, history, or sociology, any subject in the ideological sphere. For that reason we don't have believers who are writers or poets. People who believed could not go abroad. They couldn't study foreign languages. They couldn't work in the academy of sciences or in cultural institutions. Only the atheists could work there, especially the atheists who held to the party ideology. Even history is distorted. For two generations students have learned that the church only spreads darkness.

We also lost our freedom. Then egoism flourished. Because without trust and sacrifice, people become egoistical. Children told on their parents. Brother informed on their brothers. One minister was afraid of the other.

In the factories, people had no feeling of responsibility. The ecology was destroyed. The culture was devastated. I am not saying that every believer is an angel, or that an atheist is automatically a bad person. I don't say this. It is possible that in a society there will be people who believe and people who don't, and people who aren't sure. But in a place where somebody tries to make the whole society atheistic, starting with the children, the whole nation becomes a society without a conscience. In these places life cannot exist.

When children are raised with a respect for God, they form a conscience. They want to live their lives with love. They have some respect for marriage, for family, towards their parents, towards truth. And for that purpose, the church is a treasure.

It is not just enough to have enough bread. I know in South America where people are poor, the first thing that has to be done is to give people bread. But if this bread is given by atheists, they would give them bread but they would take their humanity away. For humans, it is not enough just to have bread. A person does not live just from bread, but from every word that comes through the mouth of the Lord. This is our experience.

7

The Professor
and
the Police

I wonder if you would tell me, within the context of Eastern Europe, how severe was the government's repression of the church in Czechoslovakia?

Except in the Soviet Union, I would say that the persecution of the church in Czechoslovakia was the most severe of any Eastern or Central European country. So we were in second place, so to speak.

But there was persecution here?

Yes, of course. I am afraid you can't understand it because you have lived for many decades, even centuries, without persecution. Ministers had to get licenses just to be permitted to preach. Then all the churches were supposed just to confine themselves to very limited church activity. Let's

Dean of the theological faculty at Charles University in Prague, Professor Jakub Trojan is a pastor in the Evangelical Church of the Czech Brethren. He was among the first signers of Charter 77. Having lost his license to practice as a minister in 1974, Trojan worked as an economist and was active in the underground church and in dissident organizations such as New Orientation. In 1969 he arranged the funeral for Jan Palach, a Czech student who immolated himself by fire in Wenceslas Square in protest against the repressive measures of the regime. Jan Palach was a member of Trojan's congregation.

say, Sunday service, maybe a little youth work and Bible work with adults. It was all the churches were permitted to do. No social activity, no political activity, no cultural activity or things like that. Just so-called religious activity, and which was, again, defined in terms of the official line. And if a priest or a pastor was not loyal to the regime, he would be put in jail for some supposed trespass. It was very, very easy to trespass the civil code. The code was very flexible. It was used by the state purposely to limit the church activities. This was one kind of persecution.

The other kind of persecution was that the children who attended the Sunday service had a harder time getting higher education. They were considered citizens of second rank, so to speak.

It was quite impossible in the Sixties, for instance, to become a teacher or a physician because it was viewed as ideological intolerable that students from a Christian background would become intellectuals of that social status.

In the Seventies, what happened to your church?

The invasion of Russian and other countries' troops into Czechoslovakia in August, 1968, was a great shock for the whole society. We had hoped that the humanization of socialism was possible at that time. But then it was revealed that the superpower would not allow us to take that independent way.

And this, of course, marked a start for further discrimination and persecution of the church. Before this invasion the church had been confined to tending exclusively to religious matters. After the invasion this confinement became even worse. The surveillance by the secret police in my country of the clergy of all churches was continuing. And there was a very strong and severe attempt to reduce the number of people in attendance at Sunday services. Parents of children, and those who were in good positions in the secular world were under heavy pressure not to attend the churches.

The church reacted at that time, which is quite understandable, with an attempt just to survive. Faced with merely surviving is, of course, not very encouraging for the future. So the church was very nervous. I speak here of my church—the Evangelical Church of Czech Brethren. But I think this was true of all churches. We were all very nervous. Some pastors lost their licenses, and the others who remained in office became

Jakub Trojan

fearful that if they stayed in contact with those who had been banned they too would lose theirs.

This created an atmosphere of fear and mutual mistrust and isolation. It was very hard to live in these circumstances.

Looking back now at the performance of the church, at least since 1970, how do you evaluate the church's resistance to an alien government? And what, if anything, must be done to enable the church to move forward?

Well, my impression, when I look back, is ambiguous. We were not as deeply rooted in our faith as we should have been. We lost, I think, much of our Christian substance. Sometimes the people in Western countries have the illusion that if Christians are living under persecution that their faith, so to speak, automatically becomes more courageous and strong. But I think it's an illusion.

You can become corrupt or your faith can flourish under persecution just as either can happen in comfort and affluence. So my evaluation is ambiguous.

I would say that some of our lay people and some of our pastors and representatives of the church went too far in their loyalty to the state, and some tried to resist. So there was a great division and almost no dialogue in between. There was an alien power that came between us, a force from the state and the Communist party. I think we must be honest and admit this.

How bad did it get?

Well, we now know that about ten percent of our pastors were on lists at the secret police as collaborators. A very slight consolation for my church is that there were other churches that were even worse in this respect. The current estimate is that there were about 140,000 people—clergy and lay—involved in this collaboration. Now there is a big issue of what to do about this. Some say we must publish this information. Others believe that if we did, it would have a disastrous impact on the families and children of these people. It is very controversial.

But I think there is a more important issue. This is that we have to detect and analyze our own sins, which are not only sins and failures in general, like all people commit, but some specific contextual sins and failures we have made. If we don't detect these failures, I'm afraid we will not be in the position to cope with future tasks and responsibilities.

Some of these contextual failures were transplanted into the church from society.

Give me an example.

Yes, I will give you an example. For instance, it was quite normal under the Communist regime—and I think you in the West would understand the evil I am now describing—that if somebody was accused officially by a state or party representative, he was lost. He had no possibility to defend himself, either in the press or on television.

This became common in the church as well. For example a group of us sent a statement to our national Parliament, defending the church and religious life in my country. We were accused by the state authorities, and instead of allowing us to explain the issue, we were silenced. We were denied any possibility to defend our position.

Now if you hear your neighbor accused, you will listen to the accusations, but at the same time you will ask, "Is this true or not?" And the neighbor should have the full right to defend himself. This was not possible. We were accused by the state that we were disturbers of the peace, that we were anti-state and anti-social by making our statement on persecution. And instead of having been protected by the church leadership, we were silenced by the church. We were unable to defend our issue or to even to explain how ordinary members of our own church saw it.

We were silenced by our own church leaders because they themselves had been accused by the state and feared if they did not admonish us the situation of the church would become even worse.

If you dared to protest against the government, could you count on anyone for support?

If there was any support in such situations, I'm afraid I would have to say that it was anonymous. People would perhaps express their solidarity in personal contact with you, but you hardly could expect to be supported by the church leadership because the church leadership at each level was just content to survival. And protest was viewed as counter-productive to survival. That was the problem.

Jakub Trojan

Going back a bit in time, what were the Communists really demanding in the '50s and the '60s? What did they want, and what was their standard for acceptable behavior by a church?

Well, the ways that the Communist regime dominated the society, in our area was, of course, manifold. They required almost absolute loyalty from the citizens to the official lines which they proclaimed as the absolute ideology. Students who would not comply with their demand ran the risk of not being permitted to obtain a higher education.

In the '60s, there was a requirement that only those loyal to Marxism would be permitted to study, for instance, medicine or to become teachers. This was very hard for our church, because the Protestant churches on the whole have a very good tradition of sending children to colleges and universities, particularly to become teachers.

And now, the blow. These children would not be permitted to go because of their Christian background. It was symptomatic, the way the churches reacted. Instead of launching protest action against this—this violation of basic human rights—they accommodated. They produced a new theology, a theology of the cross: Jesus Christ's cross calls us all to accept suffering and to endure the suffering.

But it was, of course, the children, the weakest among the church members who had to take the cross. And this is what I would identify as a false theological attempt to cope with the severe conditions we had to live in. Our faith was changed, not as an expression of our protest, but as an expression of our accommodation to the conditions we lived in.

In this struggle between compromise and courage, I'm surprised that the church didn't do better than society at large. What does one learn from that about conscience?

Well, we are dealing with very subtle things concerning conscience and behavior. It's very difficult to talk statistically. I would admit, and I do believe, that even in the time of persecution, there were honest church members and pastors who didn't make a lot of compromises. So I cannot make a sweeping assessment of how we behaved.

But personally, I was struck and appalled that after I lost my license, suddenly I was very isolated. I expected that as a Doctor of Divinity I could serve my church, if not as a preacher, perhaps as a translator of some textbooks or in some other facet of the educational process, but this is not what happened.

I became just an ordinary church member and I had to earn my money at another job, not as a theologian. I was practically cut off from any church activity. This was, of course, very hard, and I must confess that the power of the regime, at this very point, was revealed to be stronger than the power of holy spirit, and stronger than the power of the community of Christians.

I am far from generalizing and saying that in all churches this same spirit of false obedience, false loyalty to the regime was the rule. We need a more subtle analysis of the past.

Was your own faith and hope threatened when you couldn't turn to the church? And what jobs did you get? How did you survive?

After I lost my license to practice ministerial work, fortunately I had another profession as economist, so I earned my money in a very worldly job. It was absolutely uninspiring. Theology is my whole life, not a hobby. Fortunately there were some people who sympathized with this and we organized seminars in Prague and in other Czech cities, and we regularly met to analyze texts, theological texts. We were supported by our friends abroad who sent teachers, pastors and professors of philosophy and theology to visit us when they could. We had a sort of communion across the frontier. It was illegal. But it began growing in many towns to the point that the regime suddenly stopped the persecution. But, for me, it took 13 years.

Is it then an accident, or an irony, that from this country, where repression has been so severe, that a new idea of moral order has arisen?

I wouldn't say this is an accident, but I believe that this moral resurrection and spiritual integrity, is what we have been struggling for in the past. It is really an old tradition in my country. I would say it goes back to the time of the Reformation, when emphasis was placed on the spiritual and moral dimension of the Gospels.

This borders on the mysterious, but I believe that the whole nation was transformed subtly at special moments during the long secularization we have endured. In the '60s, just before Prague Spring. And then

Jakub Trojan

in the second half of the '70s and throughout most of the '80s. These changes took place in the reality of moral awareness, the so-called non-political politics that Václav Havel has several times emphasized. But I think this phenomenon is rooted in Reformation times.

Again, could you tell us how you lost your license?

Yes, I lost my license to do ministerial work in my congregation in 1974. I think the way I lost my license was typical of the whole situation at that time in the country. My superior in the church was sent a letter from the state officials saying that I should be removed to some other congregation, which is in violation of our church constitution. The senior could not do that.

I tried to defend myself. I appealed to several state officials, but it was in vain. My congregation appealed, nothing happened, and suddenly I was dismissed and I had to find another job. There was no legal procedure I could use to defend myself at that time. It was typical. No reasons given and no possibility to defend oneself.

Then, of course, I went to a secular job. I spent a year or two there. Then came Charter 77, and as I was among the first signers, I was expelled, of course, from my job and I had to find another one.

This was not easy. After trying 30 different companies, I eventually found another job where I spent the ten years.

I'm not quite clear. Did the state take the license? Did the church take it? Was there no reason given whatsoever?

No, there was no reason given for this attack. And the church leadership on the highest level tried to do its best by sending in some protest, but there was no response, practically. All I can do is guess why this was undertaken against me.

It might have been because I was involved in a non-conformist group called New Orientation. We tried to combine the message of Gospels with our social, economic and political responsibilities. The idea was to confirm that the gospel concerns all spheres of the social life.

Or it might have been because I arranged for the funeral for Jan Palach.

For those who don't know, please explain who was Jan Palach?

Jan Palach was a young student who burned himself in Wenceslas Square in January, 1969. He was a member of my congregation and I arranged a funeral for him and I delivered a sermon. He killed himself as an attempt to demonstrate that there are some issues in our life that are so high in value, that they demand the highest sacrifice of human life. He put fuel, benzene, on his body and then lit it. In a minute he was in flame. It was a big fire. After four days of great suffering he died in Prague Hospital.

In doing so, he revealed that politics has deep human dimensions that transcend the technical politics of daily life. It had an enormous impact on all of us, on the politicians, theologians, church members and non-believers, just to realize that, if a young man sacrifices himself, what shall we do in our daily life?

His sacrifice was a continuous appeal to us to question how we live, and ask what are the highest values of life. Politics in the end is not a matter of just the technical organization of communitarian life, but has this deepest human dimension.

Is it an accident that in this land where a dual standard, a kind of duplicity became a survival mechanism, that suddenly out of this moral vacuum the country selected a man like Václav Havel who's become an international symbol? Is that an accident or an irony?

I wouldn't say it's an accident—that a man like Václav Havel has been elected President. He was, from the very beginning, familiar with the moral and spiritual traditions I tried to describe.

I remember that he gave a paper to our pastors 20 years ago–toward the end of the Prague Spring. Despite his Catholic background, we saw eye to eye. He was excellent. We were all thinking on the same line, emphasizing the moral dimension and spiritual responsibility we have for what we are doing.

So it's quite logical, and hardly accidental, that he was involved in the Charter 77 movement with all the moral dimensions involved. He is highly appreciated in the church.

There is an irony, of course, in that he seems now to be highly appreciated in the churches and in the public who were not quite as enthusiastic on his behalf in the times of the persecution. But that may be understood in the context of the duplicitous way of thinking that you alluded to. There has been a very dramatic struggle within the soul of

Jakub Trojan

Czech people.

Sometimes the moral dimension is victorious. Sometimes the adjustment and accommodation is victorious. But which nation in the world is exempt of this duality?

Our church, the Church of the Czech Brethren, now feels a great urgency to serve its nation. I believe that eventually we will succeed in overcoming our very controversial past. But the way of moral education is slow and long. The lusts to be faced are so enormous, and failures we made in the past are so heavy and far reaching that I am afraid the way in the future will not be easy. The devastation has not been only economic or ecological. It is moral and spiritual.

If we do not overcome our failures of the past, I am afraid we will not be in the position to enter the future. I think Christianity only truly flourishes when Christians are resolute in their endeavor to undertake the spiritual struggle. We should not be lost in our sins and failures of the past.

Pastor Kocáb:
When Someone Tries to
Survive, He's Dead

What happened to churches here under 40 years of Communist rule?

Well, the most important thing was the pressure of the state against the church. The state had almost all the power in its own hands. The state tried to make the whole society conform to their ideas.

    Such a society hasn't existed in the last two thousand years in Europe. Because they had all the power–political, economic and ideological or religious, if you will–in their hands. The church had to confront this power.

    Because the Lord of the church is Jesus Christ, and we have quite

Alfred Kocáb, a senior pastor in the Evangelic Church of the Czech Brethren, was a signer of Charter 77 and suffered the suspension of his license to practice as a minister.

another interpretation of the world, it happened that the pressure of the state was especially very great against the church.

There are two important points which you must understand. The first thing is that the Communist system was pragmatically an atheistic system, and they taught in schools and everywhere else that no God exists. This, of course, was an attack on the roots of our existence.

The second thing is that because the Communists had all the power in their hands they could prevent us from working outside of the church. We were essentially confined in our buildings.

These two great dangers influenced the population very much. Atheism became strong in the country and priests faced the choice of surviving in the church or going out with the message and endangering his career and his own family.

The message of Jesus Christ is so important for the world that a lot of Christians didn't accept that his existence can live only in the church, and they tried to take it outside, but that was the reason they suffered.

How did the state impose its control on the church?

At first the control started when somebody wished to study and become minister. He had to get permission from the school where he studied. Then he had to get permission from the state. And then he could begin to study if he finally got the permission from the church.

Then afterwards, when he finished, he had to get a license–only a minister who got the license could work in the community. He was paid by the state. The money the church got from its members was under the control of the state. How the money was used was also controlled by the state. If a minister did something that was not allowed, if he organized, for instance, meetings in houses, he could be imprisoned.

What was the worst the police could do to a priest or a pastor?

I forgot to mention that the stated plan of the Communists was to destroy the church, and they said this openly. It was their program from the beginning, for 40 years. Therefore they for 40 years of this century attacked the Catholic church, not the Protestant church or the smaller ones so much. Thousands of priests have been imprisoned. Many of them died in prisons. This is necessary to understand.

Their system lasted forty years–a long time. For me, it's very difficult

Alfred Kocáb

to remember everything, because we are living in the present days with our problems and our sufferings. We already have forgotten, otherwise we couldn't live. You can't always remember what happened.

But the most difficult thing and the most terrible thing was that under this regime even our ministers lost hope. Imagine, you start your work, and slowly it is beginning to flourish, and then sombody comes and destroys it.

You do this once, twice, three times. You have to be a saint to overcome these things. To start from zero again and again. You can well imagine it would be difficult purely on an economic basis. But I am talking about working with people's souls, with their lives. You have to have a deep faith in God who is so strong that He can resurrect people from the dead. To believe and to remain firm for the long run, this was the most important thing, I would say.

Did you ever almost lose hope during these 40 years?

Yes, of course, of course, of course. I was near. I never lost it, but I was near. I'm quite a normal pastor, you see—I mean a normal man. And I have quite a simple faith, like my mother.

After the Second World War in '45 I almost lost faith because I saw that the Christian church didn't act enough against Adolf Hitler. I was 20 and I felt that I had lost my faith. I lost my understanding of the people around me, not only my enemies but even the people in my church. I lost trust. But then faith came back to me when I was 25. I had gone through a valley.

How did the Evangelical Church do in the face of this new totalitarian threat over the last 40 years?

You can't find a simple answer, because you never can say the church did this or that, because the church is divided into many groups. It is like a body, you see, or a lot of bodies. But, in general, I would say that God is stronger than all his enemies. God was merciful and he gave us enough of his spirit, that we could overcome. The greater part of the church, the members of the church, remained in the church and helped to save it. Only a small part left the church or started to collaborate with the Communists.

Tell me more about the tension between what is safe and what is right.

My opinion is that the life of church, and the life of society is one whole. Because we are living in one world, not in two worlds. And therefore, in this time when everything is in danger, our whole civilization, we are in the deepest crisis of our history.

So it is necessary to find out what the Christian faith can give to save this world, this civilization. And to find what can unite us, the Christians and atheists, the Christians with the Muslims, and Hindus, and so on. Nothing is more important than this. Christ is our shepherd, who gives his life, with no conditions. So we have to be for all. In this terrible time of the Communist system, we tried to live just for ourselves, to survive. We have learned that when somebody tries to survive, then he's dead.

We can't survive. We can only live together. Live or die together. But to stay together forever, this is Christian faith. It may be possible to save this world. But this is only a probability because we are very far on our way to destroying ourselves.

We have to find what unites us. And this means that we have to work on all the errors that currently exist, but the church has to find the well, and to stay on the well, where the water of life is coming out. This can only be done by people who have spiritual interest, who understand that humanism and the thoughts which are coming only from our own personalities are not enough.

We have to ask everybody and everything, angels and God, to help open the gates to the future.

But I know there are people in your church who say, in order to move forward, we must look at the past, we must discuss it, get it out of our systems. What about this?

Oh, this is, of course, necessary. But it's very complicated. Every society, and the church as well, must from time to time ask itself what has this organization or church done. To find a way of cleaning its own body and soul. We know it with Christians, that without this cleaning, we can't go forward. But how to do it? Normally the best way is for everyone to stand in front of his God and say what he has done. That's the normal way. We can't confess things on the public square. But there have been sins committed, sins which have been more than sins. Crimes. And there

Alfred Kocáb

is a problem as to what to do. I think that we have to combine this first method of interior penitence, with a public penitence. We have to find out where the church did bad things, and the certain representatives of the church who did them.

And we have to articulate, to say quite clearly what has been done. This is the first thing. And the second thing is that if we find somebody who is responsible, he has to find another job, because if your mistakes are too great as a minister or as representative of the church, then you have to understand that only resignation is possible.

Resignation is not death. You don't die. But it's a sign of a new beginning.

And what were the crimes and the mistakes that the church may have to face up to?

The worst was to actively collaborate with the state police and give them information about church to help the Communists undermine and destroy the church. That's the first thing. The second dangerous thing was that some of the main representatives of the church agreed with the Communist policy that church has to live only within its own walls.

This means that they betrayed the command of Jesus Christ to go to all nations with the mission of the church. These people didn't admit that they were acting out of fear. They said this is the right explanation of the Bible and this was a great mistake. And there is a third thing. The pastors and also the laymen who came into conflict with the state have not been defended. They participated in political activities, Charter 77 and so on, they had no place in the church.

How did you deal with the conflict between what you wanted to do in your heart and what the state would punish you for?

Well, it's a paradox when I look back. I think it was one of the best periods of my life, because it was one of the most difficult. God permitted me to get through it and that meant that I could reach a certain deepness of experience that will help me surely till to the end of my life. I was 48 years old and I was a rather successful pastor and, then, everything was destroyed.

This is a real test for a Christian. He can begin to really believe in God because God is now everything for him, because he lost almost everything else. A certain stability of mind is necessary to become a teacher of the gospel, because teaching the gospel is not only a matter of knowledge. It is a matter of real stability in God. People come to you because they are trying to find something that is truly stable.

So this period gave me a time to find a great amount of the fresh water of life. And from that I can now work, full of gaiety and hope.

Can you tell me what was the worst thing that was done to you by the Communists?

Well, you see they took away my license to work as a minister. They told me, "Don't preach. Don't work in the church. Leave the parish." This was for me the worst thing in the world.

Once they destroy your work and your communication with other people, you can lose your faith and then you can go to hell. And this was the right way to hell. It was their aim. Because they could give nothing more than hell, not being able to give anything of God.

So it became a fight between hell and heaven for me. I had to overcome and to win this war so I can now fight another thousand years. I have time now. Without end.

And did your church help you when you were alone? Was your church behind you?

The official attitude was not a good one. My boss, that was like a bishop, you see, said be quiet and do nothing. And I said, I am not a dog. I am a servant of God and I have to speak. And so, I worked four years in my parish even though it was prohibited by the state. I could have been punished and put in prison for two years. But they didn't do it, the Communists. I worked from '74 till '78. And then I continued as a worker. I never shut my mouth, because a servant of God who shuts his mouth will be damned by God.

I am afraid of God because I love Him. And therefore, I spoke. And now I speak more and more.

And what role did your church play in pushing out the Communists in 1989? Was your church an important part of that opposition or not?

Alfred Kocáb

Well, the attitude of the synod or council changed in the last two years a bit, but it's not possible to say that they did very much. But some members of the church were very active. Young people, you see.

You mentioned that when your license was taken away, and when you signed Charter 77, you were told by your church that this was wrong.

Yes, you know your enemies, and you don't expect much mercy from them. But it's another thing if your friends don't understand you. This is more difficult.

The leaders of my church never said that we were not pastors anymore. They said, well, all right, you have no license. Then please don't be active in the church as ministers. And as laymen, stay only on the lowest level, because there had been a special announcement that pastors who lost their licenses couldn't be elected as laymen to higher administration councils. So even according to the church law, we were imprisoned in a corner of the parish.

The synod or council asked us to undersign a paper, with a promise that in future, we will not interfere in political affairs of the country. They said if we did, we would have a chance to go back to the pulpit. But we said, no.

If a fellow pastor in your church had collaborated with the secret police, what would you do about it? Can you forgive him?

It's very complicated. We are now faced with this problem in the whole society. For instance, it has been said that current representatives of the parliament have been collaborators of the state police. But there is no legal basis for these accusations, which means that if somebody is accused he can't defend himself.

The same thing is with people in our church. We know several names, but we don't know how deeply they collaborated, or if they really collaborated. We have no real proof. At the moment, we can't see the secret papers of the state police. Only a commission in the parliament can do that. So, we are on a very complicated level. I would say the best thing is to forgive. Those who really collaborated should leave the church voluntarily and then start again.

You have talked about a combination of expectation and enthusiasm, blended with pessimism, as a characteristic of the spirit of this church. Tell me about this philosophical duet.

This, too, is a difficult issue. But a very common one in the life of individuals and communities. If God gives you too much, then you don't realize very much. The whole history of our church is, on the one hand, the awaiting of great events, which are coming from God.

On the other hand there is a certain despair, because it seems the kingdom of God is not coming so quickly. By nature ours is a nation of great expectations and also of great despair.

We have much to learn. This is a practical period after a time when we almost lost all our hope. We found hope again in the revolution. But now, we have to go forward more slowly. We have to move step by step in the church and in society. This is the great challenge for the Czech nation, the Czechoslovak Republic, to learn to live practically, step by step. That's all I can say.

The Actor: Between Good and Evil, the Border is Liquid

In Poland and Germany it was the churches that provided refuge for dissenters. In Romania it was the streets and basements. But in Czechoslovakia the theaters were also havens. Why was this?

Czechoslovakia–and Bohemia especially–have a history like that. A special history. In our country theater played a unique role, more political than cultural.

In the last century the National Theater was built. It was built by the people of Czechoslovakia from their own money–collected one crown after another–to have their own theater in the Czech language.

The struggle for national identity in this country–for a national conscience–was a struggle for language. And in this dream there was a big role for theater. This has been a tradition in Bohemia. Especially in Bohemia.

Tomas Töpfer is an actor who lives and works in Prague. He helped to organize the actors' strike of 1989 in protest against the beating of student demonstrators. This strike, and others like it, provided critical momentum for the November Revolution which resulted in the overthrow of the Communist government in Czechoslovakia.

On the stage of our theater many historical things have happened. One of them was this revolution—or change. I don't like the word "revolution." It wasn't revolution in the proper sense, it was social change.

But tell me more about why the theater has this special role in Czechoslovakia, like nowhere else?

In Bohemia, in the last century there was a great struggle for national culture, national identity. And the struggle was over whether the language of Bohemia would be the Czech language or the German language. This struggle played itself out on the stages of our theaters. The Czechs built Czech theaters— even in villages and small towns. And the Czech language was the language of these theaters.

So it's not by chance that in 1989 the theaters had a special role to play, again, in the struggle for change.

What happened in the fall of 1989? Why after 40 years of acquiescence and anguish did everything suddenly burst loose? What happened here in Prague?

Here in Czechoslovakia people say that we have suffered a totalitarian system for 40 years. This is true. But unfortunately, for those same 40 years, the same people who live here now participated in that system. Some more. Some less. We now talk about the borders of conscience. What people can tolerate. But the borders of conscience are very . . . you can move them.

Of course, events in Czechoslovakia are connected with events in all Europe, but what happened here is that people lost their patience. They had been on their knees by themselves, participating in totalitarianism. We voted. A majority of us voted. We knew it was nonsense, but we were afraid. Afraid for our children. The system, you see, was very effective. It made us feel that they could injure our children. And whoever has children is fearful for them. And that is the main reason people went along with the regime. Still this was collaborating.

Now, I am an actor, and the actor has a very strange profession. The actor works with his own body and with his own soul. His body and soul are tools. Some artists work with a material and make a sculpture or a picture. The actor is the producer and, at the same time, the product of his own work. And that's why he always connects the result of his own work with his personality.

This happens to him and also to his audience. They connect his stage personality and opinions with his real personality. But, of course, in reality these needn't be the same. Most actors don't want to present opinions they don't agree with. But when your are serving an evil, finding the border between it and what you truly believe becomes very difficult.

If good and evil could be easily separated we would all be heroes. The border between good and evil can be very liquid. It can eat at you slowly. For an actor, it is inside him, and the more he accommodates it, the more it becomes him.

It is my fear that my generation cannot feel liberty. We are like Moses' nation going through the desert. When the Promised Land was reached, the old generation was dead and only new people could inhabit the new land.

How did you deal with this problem, as an actor and as a citizen?

Under the Communist government it was not difficult to get work as an actor. If you joined the Communist Party, all the gates were opened. The gates of many theaters and, of course, television. This was the path taken by many of my colleagues.

Unfortunately for them, the national audience could tell what they had done. When they started to lie before the audience, their faces vanished. Their personality vanished. They became schizophrenic. Actors saying one thing and thinking something else.

Were you able to avoid this?

I studied for my career in the period when Russian tanks were here. These were the tanks that installed the Communist puppet government— Brezhnev's government. I entered the theater in this period. I studied hard in school and wanted to do my job.

This may be hard for you to understand, but at that time the state had an absolute monopoly over everything. Nothing private existed. No private employer, no private theater. If any one was in opposition to the state, the state prohibited him from even earning a living.

One man was powerless before this great power. But the power could be successful only as long as the people feared it. When people lost their fear, the government was powerless. Then even the secret police were powerless.

In my case it is absurd to say that I really had power. I really had fear. I admit it. I was like a small bird. I was hiding my face until–until my children emigrated. And when I lost my fear for them because they were able to emigrated to a free country–the United States–then I lost my own fear.

What happened in November of 1989 that made the bubble burst?

Well, at that time, the violence of the police, and the special units called red berets, was at a height, as was the power released by the demonstrations of student with candles and flowers. These students were brutally attacked and beaten by the special units of police. The attacks were so brutal and unexpected.

Then my colleagues were collected by phone and asked to sign some petitions against the violence that were published in newspapers abroad. Some were afraid to sign but other did not have fear, and signed the papers. But all this was only a sub-step.

The government was unmoved by these petitions. So we realized that we must gather together, perhaps in the theaters, and do something. For my part, I went to a friend, an actor, and told him to sit down at his computer and we would write a new proclamation. I knew it had to be new because there were so many of the old petitions and proclamations that had had no effect. So I dictated to him a new proclamation that called for a strike in the theaters. He laughed and said, "Oh dear, this will cause a shock that we will not survive." But he went ahead anyway. And he coded the message in the computer so that it did not use the actual word "strike" — to be careful of the police.

But it was clear to those who read it. We would close the theaters, and we would use the theater space as a public space for free discussion. This, I must say, was in some ways an absurd idea, but in some ways, not so absurd.

You see, the press was tightly under the control of the government. Television, too, was under control. Everything was. But not theaters. You could by a ticket to a theater, go in and see what was there. It was harder to control centrally. Also, our plan was not suspected.

Tomas Töpfer

So imagine. We gathered on an afternoon in the State Theater. We announced that all the theaters would go on strike. And, more than that, we all agreed that we would support a general strike.

This plan worked. It worked because it was not just another petition. It was a concrete thing that called for action. And it happened.

One knows when one is near a historical event. When you have said something, and you really believe that it will happen. One week later, for two hours, all the Republic stopped in a general strike. It was delirium. I felt that I had been a small screw in this great machine.

What happened the first night of the strike? Did people come to the theater expecting to see a play?

The feeling was great. You stand in front of people who came to see a normal theater piece, and you tell them that there will be no play. Even though the theaters were never very close to the regime, it was still a shock for the audience.

I was very nervous myself when I started to speak. But I told them they would not see a play. And I told them that we were calling on them to participate in a general strike. I was very pale. My voice was shaking. I was afraid. No one knew what would happen. Had I known the outcome I might have been steadier, but this — this was a premiere.

You know, our State Theater is a big one. There are 800 seats. All our company was on the stage. There was some old scenery behind us, but we were in street clothes. When we told the people that we would not perform that night, we did not know what would happen. All 800 people stood and began to clap. And then we sung our anthem. I do not remember everything. I was in a trance. But I will say this. That night was the last turn of what we call "the change." We were at the end. For 20 or 30 years there were so many brave people who had resisted the Communist regime. Many were in the prisons. They experienced a feeling of change in their cells. For them it was not the sweet feeling of change that we felt that night. Maybe we brought it to the last turn, but they started it in motion.

For yourself, what was the dividing line between what you felt inside and what you were willing to do in terms of taking action–public action? I don't mean in November, but I mean in the years prior.

We lived in a strange country. A country where the secret police had perfect order. But the border between simply resisting the regime and actually being an enemy of the regime was very fluid. On several occasions I had contact with the secret police. Four or five times they interrogated me. They followed me in cars.

But I wasn't really a dissident. I was trying very simply to be a dull man who was not doing anything. I was afraid and I was hiding in the face of conflict. I wanted no confrontation.

But the secret police forced me into confrontation. They forced me to be the enemy. I was afraid to sign Charter 77, for example, which called for the government to follow the human rights code of the Helsinki Treaty. All of the first 280 signers of the Charter were in prison. I was afraid to sign.

It is, I say, a very fluid border. I didn't sign the Charter, but I did try to collect money from my colleagues for those people who lost their jobs because they had actively protested against the regime. And just that was enough for the secret police to start caring about me. After a week of collecting money, I didn't have my job.

But even that was not a black and white thing. I only lost my job in television. And they refused to let me perform on stage in other cities in Bohemia. But in Prague where I had a long contract, I continued to work. My wife, who had small children, and wanted to work, couldn't find a job.

What was the most difficult thing for you during this time?

As I have been saying, the border between fear and conscience is slim and liquid. People go to the cinema and like to follow stories in which the line between good and evil is very clear. In real life, it often is not. For me, distinguishing this line, knowing truly when a man is doing good or in some way helping evil was the hardest thing.

I was no hero. I was participating in the system. And every day I had to decide how I could avoid furthering it and at the same time live a decent human life.

For example, I recently discovered one of my friends in the theater was collaborating with the secret police during that time. He must have been under great pressure. He was telling them about me. I haven't seen him since that time and I am afraid of our meeting. But I don't feel anger. Because I personally know what this pressure can do to a man. There are

Tomas Töpfer

people who now talk about their courage. After the battle they are generals. But many of them never had to face up to such pressure. But even the pressure I faced was so small compared to what Václav Havel faced that I am ashamed even to speak of it.

Who was Václav Maly? And did he play any significant role in the events of November?

I saw Václav Maly for the first time at Letná Stadium. He was a priest. I didn't know him before and, I believe, only a few people knew him. But suddenly this man appeared at the stadium—a huge place where Communist celebrations were held—and he started to speak to a crowd of a million citizens. He moderated a meeting of a million people. It was like a miracle. And then, after the revolution, he simply returned to his privacy, to his job of being a priest. He must be a great man.

Has your Jewishness and your treatment as a Jew informed any of your behavior throughout the last ten difficult years?

I was born as a Jew. You cannot choose. It is given. I was not educated to a Jewish faith. I was educated in a family who got rid of the Jewish faith; I was educated as an atheist. If being born a Jew has had any influence on me, it mainly that my family always reminded me that anti-Semitism exists, hidden and also public.

I will say I am a Jew. But when there is a time when there is no anti-Semitism, being a Jew will be not important for me, because I don't know anything about it.

Was there enough of a Jewish community left in Prague, or in all of Czechoslovakia, to be a force in opposition or not in opposition to the regime?

The state police and the Communists party were afraid of Jewish influence. It was sometimes enough just to visit the Jewish City Hall, which I sometimes did to join in some celebration. (I cannot even pray.) But this was enough to attract the attention of the secret police. And in the end, after the revolution, it was proven that the only rabbi in Czechoslovakia was collaborating with the secret police. Here it is clear what an incredible power the secret police must have had. If they managed to break the one and only true sacred Jew. Now Prague will have a new Rabbi, a well-known writer returning after years of emmigration, a graduate of a theological faculty. He will be our rabbi.

What is happening now emotionally after 40 years necessary duplicity and lying. Will that vanish overnight or is there a legacy of fear?

I'm really not sure if our generation can learn how to live with freedom, because freedom, as I imagine it, is a very tiny flower. You have to be very careful about it. And people who have been educated only in non-freedom can hardly think in a free way. Maybe they will learn how to behave like free people. But to truly think as free people, I think they must be born into such an atmosphere.

We all have this disease. We have this disease in us and it can't be healed. Somewhere in our genetic code is this non-freedom. The Communist regime caught people in its nets and made them think like slaves. Once you have collaborated, you are ashamed for what you have done, and if you are ashamed, you are not free.

I am ashamed for myself. I cannot be completely free. There are so many things I could mention, but, for example, take the elections we used to have. These were not real elections. You simply threw a preprinted ballot for a preselected candidate into a box. If you did not do this you were identified as a person who stood against the regime. I was afraid. I had little children. I am ashamed to say that I went to these elections. I must say that I had a friend who also had children and yet he refused to go to the election. And he said, "I cannot go to the election, because I have children." I envy his courage. I will live with this shame, but I hope that the next generation of our children will have the chance to know only freedom.

Russian Army overcoats hang in effigy over the main street of Prague.

"All faith is simply the orientation of a human life to the coming future."

Ladislav Hejdánek

The pink tank in Prague. David Cerny, an artist, painted the tank pink. The city government ordered it to be painted it green. Then some members of the parliament decided to paint the tank pink again in support of the painter. It became a symbol of human freedom

Cardinal Korec blessing a child in the Slovakian town of Solcany.

A graveyard of Stalinist statues. Burlap bags cover the faces of old symbols of fear and repression.

"It is my fear that my generation can't feel liberty. We are like Moses' nation going through the desert. When the Promised Land was reached, the old generation was dead and only new people could inhabit the new land."

Tomas Töpfer

"One day, the highlanders simply defied orders and went into the mountains. They took their sheep. The sun began to rise, and they began to sing."

Father Jozef Tischner

The mountain mass near Zakopane, Poland.

*The Popieluszko shrine.
The assassination of
Roman Catholic priest
Jerzy Popieluszko in 1984
was a clarifying event
that struck into the
hearts of the Poles. This
portrait hangs in his
former church in Warsaw.*

*"If Jerzy Popieluszko had been a politician, he would not have been so
dangerous. But as a humble priest, spreading
the gospel, he had to be put away."*

Michal Czajkowski

Dietrich Bonhoeffer's cell at Tegel Prison in Berlin.

Makeshift altars, such as this one in the cellar of a Warsaw Church, served as quiet gathering places for thoughtful discussion. In Poland, the Church's space became a public space where people could exchange political, as well as religious views.

The Dominican Monastery in Cracow, the home of Brother Giertych.

Father Jozef Tischner singing with shepherd children in the Tatra mountains, Poland.

Widows in Solcany , Czechoslovakia

First Communion. Okopy, Poland

"God lives in the mountains. The people lean on God every day."

Father Jozef Tischner

Tatra Mountains, Poland

Solcany, Czechoslovakia

FAITH UNDER FIRE

II

Poland

Bujak the Worker: Co-founder of Solidarity

How did you become part of the opposition movement?

Well, it was in 1979, and I was working in a very large factory, a tractor factory, and I became aware that the activities of the Communist party were destroying the factory. I could feel it and I could not accept it. I had to do something.

What were your first steps when you started to take action?

In those years, when one wanted to work in the opposition, you had to face being thrown out of the factory and having no work. You could go to prison, and leave your family without any sources for life. So you had to think how to deal with that.

Zbigniew Bujak, pacifist and factory worker, helped to found the Solidarity movement in Poland. Because of his anti-Communist work he was forced to live underground for four years during the period of martial law. A practicing Catholic, he is concerned about the way the church has engaged itself with political issues.

95

Are there other possibilities for earning money, of working? Are there other people that you can count on? I found such people and these were people from a certain organization. In those times knowing that such people exist, made me feel safe and I made a decision to act.

Was it easy to make contact with the opposition? Did you have to have someone to contact them for you?

Yes, the decision was one thing. Then there was the question of how to connect with these people who work in the opposition, who edit underground newspapers. I started to think, are there people that I could contact. And I remembered listening to the sermons of a priest, Kantorski, in the town that I lived in.

I thought these are not usual sermons. These are sermons which are based on the underground press and when I met, I asked him, if he would give me some of those papers. I said it was because I can hear in your sermons that you use that press. He looked at me very long and he knew my family. He knew that my father was a member of the AK. Then after thinking a little about it, he gave me the papers. He also made contact with the people at the press for me.

The AK, or Home Army, was the Polish anti-Communist army that fought with the German's against the Russians in World War II.

When martial law was imposed in December 1981 was there any question in your mind that you were on the right track?

This was a period of great uncertainty for me and, each decision that I made, I knew a very good step towards a good future. The most difficult decision for me was planning my time to be active. How much time do I have to be in the underground? Is it going to be a month? Half a year, or maybe a year, or maybe longer? I started to make a calculation for myself. And I came to a conclusion that in Warsaw every 20th person is a Communist, is connected with the police, with the secret police, with the Party.

I started thinking, that if this is so, then is there any chance to be active for the long run. Won't the police catch us sooner or later? And then, after thinking, after considering, and after talking to other people, I came to a conclusion that it might be possible, and so I made my decision.

It would be a long fight for survival I realized, not a quick gunfight against martial law. We had to create a large lobby that would support

Zbigniew Bujak

Solidarity abroad, and this succeeded.

For me it was really an outlet for a natural need, a need to fight. I am not a supporter of military solutions. But these things are connected together.

Did that moment ever come where your own conscience starting saying, "Am I asking too much?"

Yes, I did have a guilty conscience at one time. It was during martial law, when we made many actions, many demonstrations. It was fighting without violence, but there came a moment when I had to summon people to go out in the street.

The police were there and many of the people were beaten up. They were shot at with gas. Not only that, there were some accidents, when people were shot with guns and killed. And then, I was terribly frustrated. It was we who had summoned these people. We made the decision that a demonstration had to be organized, so we had the feeling that we were responsible for the death of these people, because we summoned them to go there.

I asked one of my friends to make an arrangement for a confession for me with a priest, and I talked with the priest about what I felt. I felt that I couldn't live alone with this dilemma. We were continuing those methods of fighting.

It was fight without violence—disregarding how the other side was reacting to it—and we won. So it could be said that this sort of justifies our decision and justifies the death of these people. That these deaths were not useless.

Did the act of confession solve your problem? Did it stop your severe doubt and questioning? Or did it come back again?

Yes, it did help. If it wasn't for that confession, for that conversation, I don't know if I would have had enough force to continue on withthe fight.

Can you give me some detail about what it meant to be an outlaw for four years? You were, I gather, the most wanted man in Poland for at least three years. How did you manage it?

The people organizing the underground had methods. Two women who were very intelligent organized a whole system of hiding. Thanks to them I survived for such a long time. I lived for only one month in an apartment and then I changed apartments.

Also, I changed my clothing, the way I dressed. Also I changed some details in my face, glasses, my hairdo. And this method worked for four years, for over four years. So I got to know hundreds of new people and new apartments, and these were people that I didn't know before.

I know, for you personally, the church played a key role, but I wonder, what was the role of the Catholic church as a symbol of opposition to the Communist government. And how did it help, if it did, the rise of Solidarity?

Solidarity was being formed as an organization, a movement, independent of the church. But the church did help. It used its influence and also its experience in social work among the people to help. So the bond between Solidarity and the church was very strong from the very beginning.

Also, the Catholic church was very open at that time. Almost anyone, a man of any religion, any denomination or faith, could come to the church and he would be received very openly. And we always felt good together. There were no conflicts. We could be together, close. Because Solidarity wasn't a Catholic movement, but it was a movement of everybody. There were Moslems there. Also unbelievers, everyone.

Did you ever feel that the church, the leadership of the church in Poland, was holding back farther than some of its clergy?

What I know from my own experience, until martial law was imposed, and also during martial law, is that there was no conflict between Solidarity and the church. Some problems sort of emerged along the way. These were problems with the hierarchy of the church. There was a moment when the church decided to treat more seriously its mission of teaching. This started to make divisions between Catholics and the unbelievers, and people of other denominations.

Solidarity never had those problems. There were just incidental incidents, a few anti-Semites—but Solidarity did not have those type of divisions. Of course, the time of divisions did come to Solidarity, but it

Zbigniew Bujak

came only after long roundtable talks. And after the overwhelming electoral success of Solidarity. It's a paradox.

Could you tell me again about that crisis of conscience that you had in hiding, but telling me in as much detail as you can about the stories on television that you saw that really braced you?

The story of the witnesses, how a demonstration looks makes a great impression, but the greatest impression on me were two films that I saw. One showed fragments of demonstrations. One was cruel because it showed a great crowd of people in front of the cathedral being beaten terribly with long police sticks. Older women were pulled and beaten. This was aggression without any sense. And this made a great impression on us.

The other film—we saw which made a great impression on us was of a police car chasing a man who was running before it. The car just hit him and drove over him and the man was killed. We knew that the man was dead. When you look at such scenes, when you look at such films, a man has to ask the question, cannot this be done differently? It is only human to want to respond with equally strong methods. Then a reflection has to come.

Violence cannot be a method of fighting and then I understood that courage, civilian courage, is much difficult, much more difficult than just courage of soldiers in war—on a battlefield.

A man wants to answer fire with fire. But then if he is a man he thinks a little. A reflection comes and he realizes that violence just breeds violence.

This reflection, this thought made it easier for us to come back to our method of fighting without violence, which, as you can see, ended in success.

After all the years of Communist rule in Poland that you have lived through, does it seem almost inevitable that soon another totalitarian idea is going to come, if one is not on very strong guard?

I have this sense that a totalitarian system like the Communist system is not going to come back because history does not repeat itself in such detail. But in different moments of history, an authoritarian, a totalitarian, dictatorial government could form.

Each time it appears, it assumes a different form in the pressure that it uses. And always you have to be on guard against that. Even now, I am afraid of that.

And what is your hope for now? What's your hunch? I know no one knows for certain, but what's going to happen here, in the next few years. Is this experiment of openness going to work after a lot of struggle?

I have many problems I cannot deal with right now. What happened to the Polish church, I am afraid is that it is intruding in political life, intruding in the President's office for example, and in Parliament, and in the works of the local and national governments.

This can lead to a lowering of the authority of the Catholic church. As a Catholic, I do not like this, because I think that in 10, 15 or 30 years, Poland will be in social disorder again.

Then a great authority will be needed to solve the problems. The church will be prevented from being that authority. Getting out of such a crisis is not only a matter of economics, but also a matter of psychology, the psychology of society.

Do you sense that the public, the general public, is wary of a larger role for the church in political affairs?

The political power of the church is already great in Poland. It is not easy for people to publicly criticize the church. I think that many people, maybe even a majority of Polish society is critical of the church. But it is difficult to be publicly critical of the church. It takes civil courage, great civil courage, and it is not easy to have such a courage.

What should the church be doing that it's not doing?

The value of religion is lowered when you teach it at school. People can be taught religion only at church, because faith is a certain internal matter, a psychological matter, which cannot take place in any place. So the teaching of religion should be done in the church.

I do see one big role for the church in Poland. There is a need for a church as a moral authority that fights intolerance towards others. Today there is a problem of people with AIDS in Poland. The church

Zbigniew Bujak

does very little to defend them.

As for abortion, if the church would just fight against it with its moral authority it would have great success. But when it tries to use governmental power and legislation, it only succeeds in diffusing its moral authority.

There is also another important issue. We're living on the edge of several cultures. On our east side, there are the members of the orthodox church. And there are Muslims who live here too, in Poland. So the church has a possibility to begin an ecumenical dialogue of understanding. And this is very important for this part of Europe.

Were you surprised by this more assertive behavior of the church, once the Communist authorities were no longer the major obstacle?

Yes, I was very surprised at the church. The church has had so many opportunities to be an influence as an authority in many fields of social life. But I think it is a mistake to use its civilian power to bring the teaching of religion to the schools. It will be very bad for the future of the church.

Have you learned anything by observing the President of Czechoslovakia, Václav Havel, a man with absolutely no training for the presidency?

I know him personally. I can say we are friends. Electing Havel for the President of Czechoslovakia is a example of Czech solidarity. I don't think it's an accident that they chose Vaclav Havel. If you knew the Czechs better, you would understand why this happened. It is very Czech in a way to elect a public person without a political history. In this sense, Havel, to the Czechs, is a professional politician. You see, I don't know who besides Havel could effect an accord between the Czechs and the Slovaks, and the Polish people too. Okay?

The Mother: If They Threw Stones at Him, He Would Give Them Bread

Forgive the ignorance of my question, but why is the 19th day of every month important?

Because on this day Jerzy was kidnapped, and the whole family's not going to forget that day.

And when did you find out that he was kidnapped?

On Saturday—Saturday, on the evening news.

And were all you—can you look at me a little bit? Can you try to look at me? It's hard. Today we saw this beautiful service in the church. Can you tell me, what was that service all about?

Marianna Popieluszko is the mother of Father Jerzy Popieluszko, a young Polish priest who defied the Office of Denominations and extended his ministry beyond the walls of his church, caring for the poor, holding services wherever people would hear them, and traveling to rural parishes to preach the gospel. He was watched closely by the secret police. During one of his trips to the country, his car was stopped by the police. He was bound, beaten and thrown into the Vistula River, where he died.

The mass was a prayer for our country.

How did this idea of a mass for the Polish Motherland begin?

Here in Suwalki, on the first month after his death, the first mass was celebrated. He wanted the mass to be celebrated in this church when he was still alive.

And did he begin the masses in his own church in Warsaw?

Yes, in Warsaw, he celebrated the first masses in Warsaw.

It has been six years since he died. How do you feel about this now?

It will never cease. The pain will never cease until I die. Where would a mother be if she wouldn't remember a son?

And who built the shrine to your son across the road?

It was built by us. It was built by us when he was still alive, but he touched it–he blessed it.

And for what reason did you build it?

It was my wish to do so, thank God. This is a custom here, around these parts. Nearly every house has its own cross outside. It means respect for the cross.

And when your children were growing up, did you have any idea that one of them would one day become a priest?

Yes, I knew, I knew. I knew about him, that he was going to be....

Let's start—let's start again, please. How many children do you have?

How much did I gave birth to or how much do I have? How many, I mean.

Marianna Popieluszko

How many did you give birth to?

Five. Two girls, three boys.

And when you had a family of five, did you expect that any one of them would ever be a priest?

Yes I did. I could see when he was very small that the Lord had given his grace to him. When he was small, he used to go to the church and serve during the mass. He would wake up in the morning very early and he knew from the very beginning that he would be a priest. He never, he never hit a bird. He loved cats—

And I heard, even when he was being watched by the police, he was even kind to them. Is that true?

I was not with him. He used to offer coffee and make coffee for the policemen who were standing outside the church. All during his life his heart was always open to everyone.

And what was it about your son that made so many people turn to him for help?

He was born on the day of the cross and he died on the day of the cross and he fought for religion, for religion to be in schools. He fought for the cross.

And if you could tell me what happened to your son? What did they do to him?

Well they—they kidnapped him, and they killed him for his faith. Each priest is an apostle, and a true priest will never abandon his own road.

How have you been able to bear the loss, over the years? Has it become easier?

How can my life be easy? I am not sure if I will even live tonight. I have never cried publicly, but I cry every day inside. My heart is sick.

Have the police made your life difficult? Did that ever happen?

No, I never had any trouble from them, even if they stopped my car on the road. When the police blessed their banner in Gdansk, a few months ago, I was invited as the Godmother of the Blessing of the Banner. I was invited by the police.

So many people have found strength through the example of your son. How do you think his life has helped other people?

His sermons were responsible for so many conversions. His message was, "Fight evil with good." No one here had that message before. If they threw stones at him, he—he gave them bread.

What is this? *(Indicating a replica of the Popieluszko monument in Gdansk.)*

This is a symbolic monument of Jerzy Popieluszko, the real monument is in Gdansk, in the Church of St. Brygida. It is very heavy. This is the way he was tied. This is how he was murdered, actually. The rope was tied around his feet and around his head so if he tried to move, the rope would strangle him.

The first night that I got it I put it in the kitchen and I couldn't sleep the whole night. I was crying. I thought he had come back to me and was showing me how he died.

Marianna Popieluszko

He's holding the cross and he's being murdered for the cross. The red rope tying him represents the way he was murdered.

12

The Dominican: The Trap Was Being Afraid

Could you help me, in the most general sense, understand what effect 40 years of communism has had on Poland.

It had a political impact, and an economic impact. But the deepest impact has been the psychological and the spiritual effect of the totalitarian regime on human choices—on the way we live out our life.

There's an analogy between the way in which the holy spirit builds charity, builds up love in the human soul, and the destruction, which is caused by human mentality and human choices, by a political system which is—which is unnatural, and inhumane.

Father Wojciech Giertych, Doctor of Philosophy, teaches theology at the Dominican Academy in Cracow. The Dominicans, based in Cracow, were especially strong in their support of the Solidarity movement. Their role in the success of the movement became critical after 1981 when the movement was officially declared illegal.

What's an example of—in daily life—of this lack of choice that you speak of?

Well, in the West, when people go shopping, the shops are full of goods. And you have to choose. And you don't buy everything. In a Communist world where the shops were empty, where people were given money by the state to prevent strikes, but there were no goods, people were accustomed to buy everything that's in the shop.

Now, when Poles travel abroad, or now that the economic situation has improved, and there are plenty of goods on the market, people feel unhappy when they can't afford to buy everything. Because they haven't learned how to choose, or how to even organize their finances well. Because they were accustomed to spend their money hastily on the mangy choices that were available.

In a general sense, can you help me understand this better.

Communism is like war. War makes good people better and bad people worse. And so this demanding situation prevented some people from growing spiritually. They don't know how to make choices, how to decide for themselves.

Certain people have become more talented, more valuable, more capable of deciding for themselves, of making difficult choices and sticking to them, whereas many people have just sort of lived very casually without learning how to mature, how to decide, how to run their lives on their own.

And now we have the situation that some people have become lost in a free society because they don't know what to choose. They preferred the cushy life that communism offered, which gave a certain stability at the price of irresponsibility. This, I would say, is the spiritual consequence of so many years of communism.

I've heard this described as 40 years frozen in time. How would you describe it?

In the negative sense there are some people who don't know how to choose, who don't know what they want, who don't know how to run their finances, how to save, how to plan, how to set up their own family life.

Wojciech Giertych

For example, young people get married, but they don't have enough money saved to buy an apartment of their own, so they live with their parents. I think people in the West mature earlier than here. This has enormous consequences on human relationships.

What role did the church play in Poland?

Well, the Catholic church was always a force in the Polish nation, where over 90% of the people are at least nominally Catholics. Catholicism was a vital force in this country at a time of a great ideological struggle. Communism proposed to set up an ideal social and political system completely closed off from any eternal values.

Thus during all these years, Christian values were present. The church always said, "This is not the ultimate world, this is not the ultimate answer that we are receiving from the Party. We have to view this world in the light of objective moral standards. Remember, we have two thousand years of Christianity behind us."

Communism's argument was that that sort of history had ended, and we were now building something completely new. But it turned out that what was being built was against human dignity, against human values, against freedom, against–against love. It was a system built on hatred, a system built on jealousy. The fact that the church said, "No, this is not it," had an important impact.

How involved were the Dominicans and you personally in aiding the opposition?

One of the tasks of my religious order, the Dominican Order, is a Christian presence in a university setting–the pastoral care of students and university professors. Now, at a time when a university was very much an institution controlled by the Communist party and used by the Party as a center for the spiritual subversion of the individual to the state, the presence of chaplains—the church—in the universities created a haven, a place where people could meet freely, could speak and discuss Christian philosophy.

We had an antidote for the Marxism which was being taught at the university. And the student chapel, where I was active, created a place where students could meet and pray and undertake a certain limited social activities, which were not controlled by the Party.

For example, we organized to help children in an orphanage, or we arranged to send food parcels to Zambia. We could do something ourselves because we wanted to do it and we were independent of any external control. Whereas all other organizations ultimately were under the control of the Party.

I remember the processions for the Feast of Corpus Christi, which traditionally went through the streets and main squares. Every year Cardinal Wyszynski insured that in every diocese and every parish a public procession was celebrated in the streets. And in the streets where you had Communist banners, where you had Communist propaganda, suddenly people would see an enormous crowd of people praying together, following the Blessed Sacrament.

This gave a sense of strength. People saw that we were numerous, that we were the majority, even though the propaganda claimed that religion would die out. In other countries, particularly in Bohemia in Czechoslovakia, where Catholics were always a minority, the church didn't have these possibilities. There, repression by the Communists was much more severe.

Can I ask you to help me with this point of the spectrum of involvement and uninvolvement of the churches in Eastern Europe. What is that spectrum and how does Poland fit into it?

The involvement of the church includes not only the political statements of bishops or the visible external activity of pastors—religious ceremonies and processions and preaching and so on—but also the individual choices of many people who witnessed Christian values and who were unwilling to comply with the obligations imposed on them by the Communists, even at the price of losing a job or losing an apartment. They paid for their resistance by the quality of their family life, or sometimes even prison, but nevertheless they remained witnesses.

Now, in Poland we had our situation which involved imprisonment in the 1950s and martial law after 1981. The rest of the time the prospect of prison was small. Whereas in Czechoslovakia, since 1949, I believe, vast numbers of Christians and of clergy spent many, many years in prison. And then when they came out of prisons they were not allowed to function as priests. They had to work in factories or do menial jobs. But nevertheless they retained their Christian identity, their personal prayer life, their witness. And this was a powerful sign to society.

Martial law was announced in Poland at dawn on Sunday, December 13, 1981. Solidarity was outlawed and 6,000 of its leaders were detained. Nine were killed. The movement immediately went underground and was sustained by its 10 million members and the covert financial and intelligence support of the Vatican and the Reagan administration. Martial law was suspended in 1983. Six years later, in April, 1989, Solidarity was legalized, and in December, 1990, Lech Walesa, the movement's leader was elected President of Poland.

Wojciech Giertych

But how did particular churches respond?

Well, we have to remember that both Orthodoxy and Protestantism in its various branches, do not have the point of reference that the Catholic church has in the Pope, in the Holy See, and in the Vatican. And this point of reference for Catholicism is always a source of strength.
Also you must remember that the Orthodox church has a tradition of subservience and obedience to a state. When the state became atheist, it became obedient to the state.

Protestantism, because it's divided and in small groups, didn't have clout. It didn't have the capacity to defend its values in as powerful a way as the Catholic church does.

How did you yourself decide in this difficult ground between conscience and compromise, between discretion and valor, how far you could go? How far you should go? You being an individual, but also part of this order.

Well, I didn't have, really, such a difficult situation because after studies I quickly entered a religious life. I didn't marry. I didn't set up a family. But I can tell you about my friends who lost jobs, who were imprisoned because they would not accept the Communist propaganda. Whereas we, as an order, well, we certainly had difficulties in receiving passports to travel abroad, receiving permission to renovate our churches, to build extensions of our priories. We had to live in cramped, difficult conditions.

We always had the fear in our pastoral care that we would have police agents come to our church to listen to our preaching or note those who participated in the activities of our student chaplains. It was very important for us not to fall into the trap by being afraid. The only way to get out of a repressive system is to not be afraid. Communism was built on fear. On a fear that is imposed on the entire society.

Once Solidarity was born and the nation discovered its own direction, then the Communists began to be afraid. It was very important that when we met with groups of students, that we not question ourselves or wonder if there was one among us who was sending off information to the police? In every group of students in a university this question was always somewhere in the background.

Now the situation has dramatically changed. The common foe has suddenly vanished. And what danger does the church now face in terms of both the challenge and the danger? I've heard there's much fear expressed about "triumphalism." What does that mean? What's involved in that?

In the last decade, after the election of the Pope, the church in Poland discovered a great sense of its own identity and its own value. It was a psychological charge for us when the Pope was elected and he came to Poland and said "Don't be afraid." This caused a psychological change. People stood up and started to fight for their dignity.

This was all done under the wings of the church, very often in church buildings with the support of priests and of the bishops. It was very easy for a parish priest to have crowds in his church when he was preaching against communism, when he allowed members of the political opposition to come and organize lectures in the church.

Thus a certain sense of triumphalism arose. The sense was that the church was a sort of spear in the struggle against communism. Now there is no common foe. Now we need a new spirituality fand a new form of prayer life more adapted to the new situation. This is the challenge now.

The church still has its supernatural mission and its supernatural vocation. And many people no longer are drawn in that direction. They are attracted by capitalism, by a market economy, by the amenities which capitalism promises. And so this is a pastoral and a spiritual problem for the Catholic church in Poland. How are we going to adapt in the new situation?

Tell me more about the danger of triumphalism for the church. Is this danger real or imagined?

Partly real and partly imagined. Under the pressure of communism the manner in which the clergy spoke to the people was not really that important because their word, which was a true word about Christian values, was accepted as an antidote against the pressure. But now that communism is gone, people are much more sensitive about the way in which they are approached.

Triumphalism is a sort of an attitude in which the priests think, "Well, we know better, we have all the answers," and as far as dogma is concerned and moral values, I believe this is true: the church has the

Wojciech Giertych

truth. But it doesn't mean that every priest and every pastoral situation is infallible. To evangelize you have to understand people. You have to be aware how they tick and you have to be able to present the gospel truths.

But there is another aspect of this contemporary criticism of the church, which is a consequence of the liberal train of thought which has come as a replacement for communism. The ultimate, I think, canon of the liberal thinking is that it's okay to look for truth and we ought to respect those who are looking for truth, but it's a sin to claim that somebody has found truth.

There are many people who reject the fact that the church sees her vocation in the preaching of moral values and the preaching of the truth that has been deposited by Christ in the church. And they feel well, now there's freedom and so the church should dismiss her vocation of preaching moral values. They call this the triumphalism of the church. Well, the church will persist in her mission even in a free society. The free society also requires the guidance and the direction which the church has always given.

Isn't there a danger that the church can move too aggressively to impose itself in a civil forum?

The church has a teaching mission, not only in the personal forum, but also in the civil forum. The church has always claimed that moral values are binding for the civil forum, as well as for the state. And now that the Communist state has fallen and we are in the process of building a new social order and a new constitution, it is the mission of the church to present Christian values and to defend them and to insure that the state is bound also by an objective moral order.

Now, this touches on questions of homosexuality, of abortion, of religious education, and the right to have an education which includes religious values. And this requires many practical decisions in education, in medical care, in social care and so on. How are these decisions to be made? These are political decisions.

The church sees the need to present these values and to insure that this state—this new state—will not be absolutely liberal and indifferent towards the values that have kept this nation going and have given this nation the capacity to persevere under the totalitarian regime.

But how far can the church go? If the church backs a political candidate, if the church makes sure certain legislation is entered, isn't that—I don't want to be overly dramatic—but doesn't this smack of some sort of totalitarianism from another side?

I think up to the moment that it was a question of abolishing the power of the Communist Party, the church gave political support to various opposition groups. The opposition that formed Solidarity, that formed the force which created the fall of communism, certainly had the support of the church. But now Solidarity has turned out to be a collection of various political options. And there are new political parties being set up.

Certainly the church is not supporting political candidates. There are so many parties that neither the bishops, nor, generally speaking, parish priests are saying, well, vote for this party, or vote for that party. There are so many parties and people can choose.

I wouldn't say that we have a case of the church using its position to support a political party. There are some politicians who would like to have the support of the church and who claim that they are setting up a Christian party, and there are many, many small parties which have the adjective, "Christian," and they would like to have the support of the church. The bishops and generally the clergy are careful not to require of the faithful that they must support this party or another party.

Another question is the question of legislation. Will the legislation of this state accept the ultimate moral values as they are presented by the teaching of the church? And here the church is trying to influence certain legislation.

A classic and a vociferous case is the question of abortion. The Catholic church does not aim to insure that every sin will be punished by the state. This is not the task of the church. The church has other means to help people grow towards goodness and towards sanctity, and that's through prayer and the sacraments. But the right to life is a fundamental issue. So in questions which are directly against justice— and abortion is directly against justice—the church would like the state to support the right to live. We support legislation that would insure that every human person has the right to live.

The question is how is this to be arranged? To what extent is abortion to be penalized? Are only doctors to be penalized, or also the mothers or the fathers or whatever? Well, this is a political question which admits various choices, various possibilities.

Wojciech Giertych

At the moment we have a situation where the Senate is proposing an anti-abortion law which passed through the Senate and has not yet passed through the Parliament. This bill has had the support of the church. But first of all, it came from the Senate; it came from the politicians, not from the bishops.

Let me ask you—I'm a Protestant as it happens, and I'm a parent, but I don't think the issue of abortion is black or white. I think it's extremely complicated; I can see both sides. But wouldn't you grant that there is more than one side to the issue, and therefore, the church can have its view, but it seems to me wrongheaded to argue that the church should be able to civilly impose its view.

As far as abortion is concerned, there is generally no doubt that a human fetus is a human fetus and has the right to live. The question—the political question—is in what way is that right to be assured? Is it to be guaranteed by the state? And here there are various possible solutions. But the church is against a situation in which the state will grant a certain percentage of people in society the right to decide about the life of other members of that society. And, and I would say even deeper, the issue is not only a question of abortion, but it's a question of whether the state in its functioning will accept an objective moral order which is binding for that state.

Your founding fathers in the 18th century had the same belief. That the civil order must respect the divine order. That's why you have the name of God printed on your dollars.

Now, in this late 20th century liberal atmosphere, I think it's important for the church to stress this. And in Polish society where Catholics are a majority, where a democratically elected Senate has come up with a bill which defends human life, it's quite natural that the church is giving its full support for this issue because it's a fundamental issue. It's a fundamental issue about human life.

Now there's a new political order all of a sudden in Poland. And doesn't the church have to grapple more broadly with its position than to assume that its view of the natural order is, in fact, the natural order? I mean, in a free society another church might have a different idea. The Quaker church in our country believes in pacifism; don't go to the army. But no one would dream of impos-

ing that as a civil statute. So at this dawning moment of another democracy in Poland, doesn't the church have to define for itself at least how far it should go?

The church cannot redefine moral values; they're given. The church reads them, and preaches them. They cannot be changed. They're objective. And this is the understanding of moral values by the church.

But the question of to what extent do we want them to influence the constitution, the functioning of the state, well here I think there are three rules.

First of all, we want evil acts that are against justice to be punished. Not acts against charity or acts against faith or against temperance. Only acts which are against justice are to be penalized by the state.

The second point is there must be a sufficient number of people in the country who support the penalization of a particular act.

And the third point is that if we are convinced that the introduction of a bill which penalizes a particular act which is evil would create a civil war—an even worse evil—then we should refrain from that.

For example, when religious instruction was introduced in the schools there was a great clamor among the media that this was imposed by the church, that it would not find support among the teachers or parents. But generally this has been accepted. There have been minor abuses here and there, but generally this has been accepted. And the parents prefer to have their children have the religious instruction in the school rather than to go out on the streets, cross the road and go to the church and have a more difficult time schedule, timetable during the week.

Now, concerning abortion. Taking into account the massiveness of the demoralization of the nation, which is a consequence of the fact that abortion has been legal since 1956, this may require a more gradual approach to the problem. And here it is possible for a Catholic to have various opinions. But ultimately the decision has to be made by the individual.

If the individual is immature and would like to throw all the responsibility on the priest in every sort of minute question, well, then we have to help him and say "No, decide on your own." And this is the role of spiritual direction, not to lead people to spiritual subservience and slavery, but to a spiritual maturity and independence.

Wojciech Giertych

Wouldn't it follow from that then, if an individual has to find his own moral way with the guidance of the church that the church might be wise to keep itself out of legislation, to inform but not impose its will in the law?

Look, we do not live on an island. We live in a society in which the state, through its various functions, has an influence on moral decisions. The state runs schools and orphanages and hospitals and has a program of family allowances and so on.

The state must know what is good and what is evil. If a headmaster of a school cannot dismiss a teacher who's a homosexual in the name of liberty, in the name of tolerance, it becomes very difficult to educate, to lead young people to maturity if the state does not know ultimately where is good, where is evil, what is natural, what is unnatural.

And so it is the job of the church to inform the state in its functioning, to teach, to keep in society an understanding of what is good and what is evil. A certain praxis has to be evolved, has to be prepared for the state. But the actual decision-making, the passing of the bill is not the task of the bishops or of the clergy, it's the task of the Parliament, of the political forces.

How tolerant are you, and how tolerant is the Catholic church of minorities, including homosexuals, minority religions, people who have diseases that aren't socially acceptable? Where does love cease and the moral order of right and wrong begin?

There are two questions. We have to distinguish between moral teaching, which has to be objective, and independent of the whims of society, and the individual case, the human person who may be a sinner, who may be disturbed, who may be sick, who may be a homosexual or whatever. The church receives every sinner and transmits the grace of Christ and the forgiveness of Christ to everybody.

And so we do not reject anybody. We receive everybody who wants to come, who needs the help of Christ. But in the receiving of a sinner we have to give him clear values. We have to teach him what is right and what is wrong. We're all sinners. So we have to have a very high moral standard. And even though we don't always live up to it, even though we fail, we ask the forgiveness of God, and we try to live up to that standard.

Can you understand how some people, maybe myself included, are frightened if not intimidated by the notion that someone knows absolutely what is good and what is evil?

I accept that it will frighten some people that the church claims that the truth in moral values— and certain dogmatic truths—have been deposited in it by God. But the church claims infallibility only in dogmatic questions and only in moral issues and only infallibility when what's claimed is the official teaching of the magisterium of the church, the Holy See, the Pope.

The Communist Party claimed infallibility in questions of economics, in questions of social politics. And virtually every decision of the Communist Party was claimed to be infallible. And that was really frightening.

Now in this new situation in Poland the church is not imposing particular social or political solutions. The church is just reminding people of ultimate moral issues, and abortion is one of them. The right to live is a fundamental issue.

I can understand that some people may claim that this is frightening—that the church believes that in these issues there is no doubt. But the church has to remind the state that the state does not have the right to kill innocent people. If we grant to the state, or if we grant to some members of society, the rights to decide on such an issue, the basic foundations of that state are being shaken.

We've had enough of a state which denies the existence of moral values. This was the experience of totalitarianism, and that's the experience of Hitler as well.

In the United States there are certain Catholic politicians who have separated their legal action from their personal belief, particularly on abortion. And yet they consider themselves loyal Catholics. Does that make sense to you?

It is possible for a Catholic to claim that abortion isn't evil and at the same time to claim that this particular evil will not be penalized by the state, or will be controlled by the state in such a particular manner, and yet remain a Catholic. St. Louis, the King of France in the 13th century, introduced prostitution, which was under the control of the state. He is a saint in the Catholic church. But as a king he felt that prostitution

Wojciech Giertych

should be under the control of the medical care of that medieval state.

It's possible also today, for a Catholic, say, a minister of health to believe that the use of contraceptives is against a development of love in married life, but at the same time to believe that it's better for contraceptives to be for sale in chemists' shops rather than on the streets.

Nevertheless, objectively, this is a moral evil. From the point of view of the pastors and of the preaching mission of the church, we have to always try to raise the standard of morality and to show that it's binding also for the state.

Is the declension between faith and morality in Poland in any way reflected in the difference between the raw, visceral faith—the peasant faith, as I've heard it called—and the more intellectual liberal understanding?

Catholicism is an element of Polish culture. And so we all breathe various Catholic traditions from childhood, from infancy. And so many people have a faith which is a traditional faith received in the way of celebrating Christmas and Easter and so on. And this is very strong particularly in the popular masses in Poland.

But that does not necessarily mean the basing of one's self on divine grace in a difficult moral issue. And so the pastoral question for us is how to help people coming from the traditional Christian traditions which they have, to a life of faith, a life of the practice of faith, which means that when I have a difficult issue, when I have a demanding situation, that I ask the help of Jesus Christ and I undertake what is morally good.

Since Catholicism is so widespread in its traditional dimension, many people are sort of accustomed to have the externals of Catholic devotion and practice. But there is a dichotomy between the faith which they declare and the way in which they live.

In Western Europe those who declare themselves to be Catholics have a higher moral standard. Whereas here, everybody's Catholic, but not everybody's living up to the Catholic ideal.

As far as the distinction between the popular masses and the intelligentsia, the popular masses have a popular Catholic piety and devotions that have persisted for centuries and that persist today. The intelligentsia has had stages of being away from the church, and in the 20th Century we've had two phases of the intelligentsia coming back to the church. One phase was in the 1930s where people of the right wing of the traditionalist nationalist parties discovered the value of Catholicism in expressing a national Polish identity, and there was a return to the church.

And then in the late '70s and in the '80s people of a leftist intellectual formation discovered the value of the church in defending human rights in the fight against communism and they came back towards the church.

But in both cases, to many people, the return was in a sense like coming to a supermarket—and choosing what they wanted, but not necessarily discovering personally Jesus Christ as a savior, as the one for whom they were redeemed.

So in Poland, conversion to Catholicism often is more of a sort of a political-sociological return to the scale of values and ideals and national identity. Or a political stance and not necessarily a deep personal conversion towards Christ.

In America, while we do have "In God We Trust" on the dollar, we've always had a tradition of separation of church and state so absolute that it sometimes seems to defy logic. Does the example in America inform you in any sense about the issue of church and state?

I think in America that your forefathers had a vivid sense that the state is dependent on divine law. And the name of God is very often mentioned by American politicians. And there is a vivid understanding that divine law is binding for the state.

How this functions in practice, well I think you know better than I do. I think in recent decades in the entire western world this dependence on the Judeo-Christian tradition which defended the role of divine law, also in the social order, has greatly weakened.

It's a problem in America as everywhere. But now that we're building the new constitution and the new political order in Poland, the church wants to keep an awareness of this dependence alive in our Polish state.

13

Mr. Kakol of the Office of Denominations

Please tell us what your job was during the years that Poland was ruled by a Communist regime. And what was your relation to the church in Poland?

I was the first director of the Office for Denominations. I was obliged to—to talk with religious organizations and help them with difficulties in the area of public life. I worked against officials, who wanted to see the churches as negative institutions, not institutions that could be negotiated with or which could be talked with and cooperated with. My job was to solve such problems with the churches and religious organizations.

I think that the biggest threat to the government was the government

Kazimierz Kakol was the director of the Office of Denominations in Poland from 1974 to 1980. Among his responsibilities was reading each week transcripts of sermons collected by the secret police. As he explains here, priests who were publicly critical of the government were often disciplined by his office.

itself. But the church was a power, a social power which criticized the authorities and wanted some modification of the policies of the state. In 1976, the church acted as a base for Solidarity's beginning and the church played a decisive role in giving birth to the child that we call Solidarity. It was not just any role. It was the deciding role. The church supported the illegal organization of Solidarity from 1976 to 1980. If it wasn't for the Pope and the Vatican, and then the happenings in 1989 in Gdansk, and the protection that the church gave to Solidarity, its success would have been impossible. Also the church's participation in the elections of 1989 was critical to the success of Solidarity.

Isn't it true that the government perceived the church as a threat to communism during those years?

Yes, it is true, and also it is not true. Because the threat, the threat was against the regime in Poland, and also the entire Polish nation. I think that many people in authority during those years understood that the nature of Poland's cultural environment compelled us to treat the church's role as positive.

Why was Father Jerzy Popieluszko perceived as a threat?

I cannot say why he was a threat. But some things are obvious. He was very popular. Many people came to him. He had a very big congregation and he gave them an ideology. His murder was absolutely irrational and cannot be explained from any point of view.

It's was a pity—oh, wrong has been done. And the people hold it against the government, the murder. The secret police did it and they broke the regime. They did not listen to their. . . . It was stupidity and anger. Popieluszko's activity could not be stopped. He represented patriotism. He spoke against the Soviet Union. He was a man of principal and he did not go for any compromise in saying the truth—in saying bad things about the government.

How did you feel about the election of a Polish Pope?

Generally, my feelings were complicated. On the one hand I felt satisfaction that for the first time in 450 years, a Pole is Pope. On the other hand, we were scared of what might happen.

Kazimierz Kakol

What were you afraid of?

Well, for the first time in 40 years, the streets of Warsaw and in all of Poland were thronged with hundreds of thousands of people gathered not in the cause of Communist government, but rather for the church, social justice, and an ideology, which was quite different from the Communist ideology.

That was the danger. The people felt their power, and individually, they had always thought what they thought. But now the government saw that there were hundreds and thousands of people that were thinking the same thing.

Personally, I did not see any evil in it. I knew very well what Cardinal Wyszynski thought and what the Pope thought. I talked to the Pope many times before he was elected, when he was Archbishop of Cracow. And I understood very well that what they both wanted was for the good of Poland. No one has a monopoly on doing good for Poland.

I was not only a member of the government, but I was also a member of the Party, the central committee of the Party. I would like to draw your attention to one point. The Polish Party, was called the Workers' Party, but it was the Communist Party. The adjective "communist" was not used.

After the Second World War, the Polish government tried to walk on its own. Gomulka was not subordinated to the Soviet Union. In 1956, a very strong controversy took place between Poland and the Soviet Union. And during the whole period of Communist rule we searched for a road which would be special to Poland. That road consisted in, for example, the idea that the church in Poland was controlled, but it was not repressed like in other Communist countries.

Wladyslaw Gomulka became the first secretary of the Communist party in Poland in October 1956. In 1970, he was replaced by Edward Gierek.

How did you view your role in this relationship? As a force against repression?

Yes, we were intent on not controlling the church, but working with it, coordinating, cooperating with it. The Central Committee of the Party was of the point of view that there had been a sort of "election by feet." The presence of hundreds of thousands of people, to see the Pope, was what we called an election by feet. We could not have a policy against a nation.

In the Secret Service and the Ministry of Internal Affairs, there was a special unit which dealt with the church and with its activities, and that unit gathered material about the church's disloyal activity towards the government. And many priests were repressed in many ways.

For example, they were not allowed to go abroad. They couldn't get a passport. Bishops, who were considered leaders of the opposition, did not have permission to build new churches, even though they expressed the need. The Secret police tried to make priests loyal to the government. I got information straight from the secret police and also indirectly. Secretary of the Episcopate Dambrowski, Archbishop Dambrowski, or his workers, came to me and told me to defend the priests, because they are being repressed. I always faced the conflict between what the secret police were telling me and what the churches were saying. And I had to reach some kind of a conclusion which would be for the general good. For example, each Monday, there would be on my desk tapes from, you know, sermons gathered by the secret police. They were listening to sermons. The sermons were recorded and then typewritten reports came to me that identified this or that sermon as being disloyal in some way.

I think this work was completely useless. But there was a difference of opinion between the secret police who recorded these sermons and the workers in my office. What I mean to say is that the people in my office tried to make their—my unit tried to act—generally. . . .

Try to explain what you mean.

Yes. The problem of disloyalty in a public person like a priest, is a problem which can be regarded in different ways. For example, when a priest criticizes social conditions, he is summoning his people, his faithful, to do the same. If he's doing it publicly, as a sermon, he is using his position and his intellect, but he's not doing it rationally.

Rationally?

He's not doing it rationally. He's not doing it rationally. He's doing it in the name of God. This, I think, is—is disloyal. If he was saying personally, "This I don't like," that is one thing. But if he says, "The Virgin Mary doesn't like it," that is too much.

When he's criticizing a law, for example, as the Bill of 1956 which allowed abortion was criticized, then he, of course, has a right to do that. He may say that the Bill allows abortions, but does not force people to

Kazimierz Kakol

have them. If the faithful are faithful to the church, then the bill about abortion will die a natural death. No one will actually have an abortion.

In this area of the public activity of priests, I think the authorities in Poland were very sensitive to criticism coming from the Soviet Union. It's a great superpower, a great friend, and criticism from the Soviet Union upset us a lot.

It was okay if it was just criticism, but not if it offended. When the Soviet Union was offended, then, for example, private citizens would go to court and sue even the church for saying bad things. This could not be accepted.

To what extent did you try to control members of the clergy?

We used the means known everywhere and in every society. We used people of weak character. We had to find certain things about a priest that he would try to hide. Like, for example, a certain vulnerability to drinking. We also had many cases of priests living with women, which is very much against the church principles. And, of course, these situations were very beneficial for us. We could discredit a priest. We could ask for the transfer of a priest to another parish. If the parish was poor, the donations would be smaller. So, of course, this kind of transfer was economic punishment.

What about sending him to prison?

Yes, in the 1950s, Cardinal Wyszynski, for example, was repressed a lot and he was imprisoned. When the priests were accused of participating in the terrorist underground in the 1970s this did not happen. Only one priest was arrested, because he was a chaplain of a young terrorist organization which killed a sergeant of the police.

But there were other ways. For example, the relationship between the Vatican and the state was such that a priest with whom the government was uncomfortable could be sent to the Vatican to study or something like that.

As for Popieluszko, there was only one way of dealing with him, and that was translocation to the Vatican. Because moving him to the Vatican would be done by the church authorities. Any other solution would mean making Father Popieluszko very important. Any other means of repression wouldn't have any sense.

Father Czajkowski: Even Christ's Death Has a Political Dimension

Father Czajkowski, I know churches have a different extent of involvement in the changes that happened in 1989. Different churches in different countries. But in Poland, can you give me an idea of how involved was the Catholic church in the movement that overcame communism?

Compared to other countries, the involvement of our Catholic church in Poland was very great. Because you know, the Polish church historically is connected with the nation. In these last years, the church had a prophetic role against communism. Also the role of comforter. But always, first of all, a religious role. And now, when Poland is again free, the most important function of the church is this religious function. Not the political function.

Father Michal Czajkowski is a professor of Philosophy at the Academy of Theology in Warsaw.

Go back. Did the Catholic church provide a safe haven, a nurturing ground, for Solidarity? Or would Solidarity be with us, just the way it is today, if the church did not exist at all?

We cannot exaggerate the role of the church, because even without the church, our people would fight for freedom. But our people are Christians, the majority Catholics, and the role of the church was very important. But its first function is religious. You know the gospel is a message of freedom. If you are a true Christian, you cannot agree with dictatorship.

This is purely religious, but the church played a special role in the grounding of Solidarity. The church is also a community. And the members of the church were also the members of Solidarity. The young people, the workers, who were prepared in our churches, in our parishes, founded the Solidarity movement.

Also the bishops and priests played a big role in Solidarity. Our Primate, Cardinal Wyszynski, and then Cardinal Glemp, helped the workers in the fight.

In Czechoslovakia, the church was not a safe haven for the opposition because the police would move in. Was the church safe from the government and from the secret police here in Poland?

In other countries, it was more difficult because the Catholic church was weaker. For example, in Czechoslovakia, the Catholic church is not the church of the majority of people. And secondly, the persecution of the church in Czechoslovakia was more terrible. In Poland, the persecution was not so great.

A church is always a free space. But here the church was really the space of freedom, where people could come to speak freely and to plan.

The police weren't as hard in Poland as they were in Czechoslovakia. Still, nothing could be harder than what happened to Father Popieluszko. Could you tell me what happened to him?

Father Jerzy Popieluszko, was my young friend. He was a good example of how the church helped Solidarity. He was nominated by Cardinal Wyszynski to be the chaplain of the workers of the Warsaw steelworkers.

Michal Czajkowski

At the time he was ill and physically very weak. He was not born as a hero. He was simply a young priest who stayed on the side of these workers. He preached only the gospel of Jesus, not politics. He collected medicines for people who were sick and shoes for children, and so on. He celebrated the mass for our country, for Poland. Many people came for these masses, believers and unbelievers. It was a sign of our common solidarity in Poland.

But he was not a politician. Not a demagogue. He was only a preacher of the gospel, and this was precisely why he was such a threat to the dictators and so dangerous for communism. If Jerzy Popieluszko had been a politician, he would not have been so dangerous. But as a modest, humble priest, preaching the gospel, he had to be put away.

Our secret police killed him. But you know, you cannot kill the gospel. You cannot kill truth. After his death, his activity, his influence, was even bigger. I was confessing people in his church after his death, so I know how many conversions we have to thank Father Popieluszko for. How many changes came from his death.

Why Father Popieluszko? Why did the nation seem to turn to him? Why him?

I think the secret of his influence, of his radiation, is God's secret. I cannot understand his secret. We had priests more engaged, more intelligent, more cultivated. But God had chosen him. Perhaps this was because his love of God and of the people was greater. He loved more, I think.

He lived not for himself, but for others. He knew that he would die. I know that, because before his last trip to Bydgoszcz, where he died, he had looked for me, but could not find me, and told his students, "Tell Father Michal, that if I do not return, he has to continue and take over my lectures and my work."

Now he showed his love, not only for the workers and students, but also for his enemies. For example, he prayed for the agents of the secret police. He offered them coffee and tea and hospitality. And I'm sure that his example and his prayers changed the hearts of many of his enemies.

You said before he was a man of the gospel and not a politician, but this can be a difficult dividing line.

133

Yes. All our life and activity, pastoral activity, has a political dimension to it. My preaching of the gospel, the Eucharist, Holy Mass, has a political dimension. Even the death of Christ on the cross has a political dimension. But you must distinguish between this political dimension of life and political engagement when you are fighting one party.

As priests we know that our pastoral activity will have an influence on political life. This is good, because we have to try to change our public life in the light of the gospel. But our goal is to prepare the heirs for the Kingdom of God, not for the church or for political life, but for God.

It's ironic, but I've been to Germany and to Czechoslovakia where the behavior of the church often hadn't been very good in the past. And now I come to Poland, where the church behaved quite well, it seems, and stood against the Communists. But here I find people worried that the church is too powerful, too triumphant. Can you explain that?

Some people in Poland who were Communists, or who served Communists, would like to have the church outside of the public life. But this is impossible. They cannot close us in the church only. Our mission is in the world, in the public life.

But there is also some fear on the part of Catholics that the church has too much influence in the public life. Some priests, perhaps also some bishops, would like to be everywhere. Our faithful invite us to every public occasion. But there is a danger in triumphalism. I see that sometimes our presence in the public life is not according to the testimony of the gospel. You know, Christ's church has to be, like Jesus, very modest, very undeserving, not looking for power for itself. But I don't think the danger is very big in Poland. The dangers of triumphalism work not only against the state, against the unbelievers, but most importantly, against the church itself.

Could you describe the legacy of duplicity and deceit that has been left in Poland in the wake of the Communists?

The legacy of the Communists in our public life, and in our souls and in our spirit, is very heavy and dangerous. It created a double truth. One truth for home, church, and friends, and another truth for public life, for work, for the press, and so on.

Michal Czajkowski

Our country is finally free, thank God. But we are still not entirely free. We now have to fight for our internal freedom. This legacy of the Communists will be present for many years, I fear. You see, during the German Occupation and later during the Communist occupation, the state here was not our state. The state was the enemy and you tried, with your intelligence, and with what capacity you had to deceive the state. For some people, stealing state property was not a sin. And now we, as the church, have to change that mentality. We have to be able to criticize the state, but we must know that it is our state.

The Pope came here in 1979, and I've heard from everybody—Catholics and non-Catholics—that this was a tremendous symbol of possibility. Could you tell me about that?

The Pope's visit to Poland in 1979 was very important, not only for us in Poland, but also for the other Communist countries, because he was officially accepted as a head of state. He could say anything he chose, and he spoke about freedom. And about our responsibility. And about Solidarity. He prepared a way for today's freedom and also for the grounding of Solidarity. Finally somebody could say publicly what we had to hear. The Pope united us. Through him we were reminded that we have behind us a long history that did not start in 1945 with the coming of the Red Army.

Our history is a history of a thousand years. And in our history, there were not only faults and errors, but also many very nice pages. We realized that this past can now act and give us strength and power for today and for the future.

The Pope spoke also about conscience. He often speaks about conscience. In fact he speaks to us every Wednesday from the Vatican and he often talks of conscience.

Conscience, during the Communist time, was largely asleep, but there were many people whose conscience was awake. And I think that this long process of renewing Poland started with conscience, human conscience, not only Christian conscience. There were always people who would not lie, who would not call black, white and white, black. It was common though to be faced with the problem of small everyday compromises. This is very dangerous for the human soul. We cannot speak only about the system, about structures that force these compromises, because in the end it is the individual who has to decide to choose.

System or structures cannot absolve you from your thoughts.

Of course, there are sinful systems, but the sinner is a man and not the system. You have to convert yourself, change your life. And men who change their lives can also change structures and systems. Changing systems without changing men is very dangerous, very dangerous. It is the case of every revolution–changing the system without changing the hearts of the people.

Was Father Popieluszko an example of a man helping to change a system?

Father Popieluszko didn't speak about changing structures. He spoke about changing human hearts. But by doing so, he changed systems in Poland. His principle was the phrase of St. Paul, from the Letter to Romans. It is difficult for me to translate into English: "Don't let evil overcome you, but overcome evil with good." And he was faithful to this. And I think that he really overcame evil with his goodness, and with the goodness of God.

It seems to me that Dietrich Bonhoeffer and Father Popieluszko are, for different eras, a little bit like one man, only in that they both believed that the church can be involved in real life, not kept in some cloistered corner. Is that appropriate?

Every prophet has to be prepared to be misunderstood in his own community. It was the case of Israel's prophets. It is the case also of Christian prophets. The German Protestant pastor, Dietrich Bonhoeffer, was criticized in his community. Only the small "confessing church" of Germany was with him.

But other Christians were against him, not only Nazis, but also good Christians. "He's going too far," they said, "His activities are dangerous for the church as a whole." And so on. Father Popieluszko was better understood in Polish society and in the Polish church. Only Communists were against him, saying that his activities were not pastoral activities but political activities.

The Polish people and his colleagues praised him and almost all the bishops were with him. They understood that his work is the part of the mission of the church. There was some opposition from the bishops against him, but it was not very important for him. We spoke often about

Michal Czajkowski

this. Sometimes he was a little sad. Sometimes he felt—he felt alone. The whole propaganda machine was against him. Television, radio, newspapers, magazines saying, "He's doing politics. He's not a good priest." This propaganda was effective in some manner, but not very effective. But that was not all he had to face. His telephone was under control, every conversation was taped. His house was also watched. His presbytery in Warsaw was also staked out day and night. There were always police cars, and policemen not in uniform who noted every person who came to him.

He was always followed. Even during his last trip from Warsaw.

What did they do to him?

I think that the police wanted to scare him and to show him that they knew everything about him. And, sometimes, to make it impossible for him to meet with other people. They were gathering evidence for a trial.

In the very end, what did they do? What happened that night?

The Communists were afraid that a trial would be impossible because they didn't have enough material against him, so they decided to kill him. So that night, during his trip from Bydgoszcz to Warsaw, they stopped his car and they tied him up and then beat him. They tortured him and they threw him into the river, the Vistula. Perhaps he was still living when they threw him in the water, but he was found dead.

And were his mother and father, these very simple people whom I've met, were they also under constant—

Not only Father Popieluszko but also his mother, old mother, old father, his brothers and sisters, his friends were always under pressure.

From this, you can see the method of the Communists. The persecution was directed not only against his person but also against his mother and father, and against his brother and sister. It was also directed against his friends.

This was their method. The idea was to frighten people. To cut them off from other people. To cut the solidarity. To show you that you are alone and nobody is with you. Then, they thought, you would have to—to give up.

Did you ever think Father Popieluszko had gone too far?

I know that some people, some friends, and also his bishop, Cardinal Glemp, asked him to stop. Cardinal Glemp wanted to send him to Rome for further studies. But I felt that he had to do what he was doing. He was not going too far, no, no.

The Philosopher: The Soul Cannot Be Killed

Father Tischner, when we first spoke and I told you I was trying to do a film about conscience and about understanding what totalitarianism meant, and you told me to come to the mountains, the mountains of Poland to see what communism had done to the shepherds here, and I wonder, if you could tell me why—why did you tell me that? What is it about this place and the effect that communism had that you thought was important for me to see?

Okay, we are in the mountains, the Tatra Mountains of Poland. These are the most beautiful mountains in Poland. The village is called Witow and the border with Czechoslovakia is very close by, but this is not the most important thing.

Of most importance is the people, people with a feeling of freedom, with their sense of humor, and also with a great sense of duty. Freedom,

Father Jozef Tischner is the Dean of Philosophy at the Papal Academy of Theology in Cracow. He also teaches philosophy at the Drama School of Cracow. He is the author of many philosophical books and appears frequently on Polish television.

which we will talk about, is not a destroying power, but a power which is building. Even when we were under communism we could see that kind of freedom.

The history of this land is sort of separated into two parts. One part after the war. That history was a history of fighting against communism until 1949. There were soldiers here in the mountains who fought against the Communists. This fight ended tragically. Many people died, many people were taken to Siberia. I could tell you a lot about that.

After that, another kind of fighting began. What kind? Please imagine a house. There's a man living in the house, together with his father and mother. Please imagine it's an old house, four hundred years old, and then all of a sudden someone—a stranger—comes and takes from the man the things which have been part of his house for years.

He takes away paintings, land, many things. What does the man feel? How do you feel when a stranger comes to your house and takes over and rules? Okay, the simplest thing is to just throw him out. But suppose he is too strong?

Different methods will be found. One solution is to fight for your right of ownership. I emphasize the word 'right' because that is fighting for something ethical, something moral, something which is close to conscience. The question then is not who controls the house, but who has the right to control it. A man can lose his things, but a right stays a right.

What happened to the shepherds in these mountains?

It was simple—and tragic. One day, people woke up and discovered they were no longer owners of the forests and valleys that they had received from the kings of Poland three hundred or four hundred years ago.

They stopped being owners. They became strangers on their own land. And they were helpless. The judge could not help them. The authorities were no help, not even the parliament, they were all Communists.

The only authority, the only force that was on the side of these people was the church. But it was a moral force. What is a moral force? Seems like nothing. The church does not have cannons or weapons. But in a country like Poland, such a force can have a great strength.

This fight cannot be seen on the outside. It happens inside, inside a human soul. So when people felt this force, when they knew they had the

FAITH UNDER FIRE

Jozef Tischner

church backing them, they started building chapels in mountains, and praying. As if they were coming back to this land through prayer. This was a very interesting road. You see, all their culture, all their music was connected with these mountains, so it wasn't only a matter of ownership but also it was a blow to the soul.

Why have you cared so much about these people?

I am from here. I was born here. My parents were teachers in this region. In a sense, I'm a shepherd too. They deal with sheep which are happy, which are polite. I deal with sheep which are so not polite, not so good. I think that as shepherds, they are better than I am, because I think that they love their work better than I love my sheep.

Why don't you love your sheep, as you possibly should?

It is a great mystery—the faith of these people is a great mystery. Faith is very difficult to understand, and what's important in this faith is its power. It could be said that God in this faith is always present. God lives in the mountains and lives close to these people.

As a priest, I very willingly take my example from these shepherds who guard their sheep, care for them in any weather. They are very heroic. This is it.

Yet you told me that one can't always connect faith and morality.

There is a relation between faith and morality. But what is it? Some moral principles are obvious, like fidelity. Here in the mountains people drink too much alcohol. They are very aggressive. Sometimes they hit each other. Often their faith takes the form of penance. When they go to church or on a pilgrimage, it is usually not to boast about how they're so good. More often it is as a penance for a sin.

There is a story here about a church that was built, not far from here, in Zakopane. The priest asked people after confession to bring stones as penance. Each sinner was to bring one cart of stones for the church.

When people heard of this they began to bring stones in advance, before confession. So in the morning the priest could tell how many people would be at confession by the size of the pile of stones waiting for him. This too is a sign of faith, a sign of faith which knows penance.

You are a man from the mountains, and you are also an intellectual. Could you tell me how do you use mountain nature and mountain faith to fuel or balance your intellectual life?

In the city, we don't know what rain is, how its water tastes. We don't know what the wind is. All this is lost. Pain here too is more real, and rest and happiness. The dancing, the language. I love the language, the dialect in these mountains.

It's an old Polish dialect. It is very imaginative, very humorous, and it always focuses on the main point. I have a certain philosophical principle that if there is a thesis which cannot be translated into the dialect of these mountain people, it is not a true thesis.

You said earlier that under communism there was a forced duplicity. People thought one thing on the inside but said another thing. Is there a legacy from this that needs now to be addressed?

This is a very painful matter. We have to remember that the basis of the Communist system that each man betrays another man. This went very deep. If, for example, you had a car, people were suspicious. Where does the car come from? Where did you get it? Illegally? If you built a house, you were under suspicion. If a policeman stopped you in the street, it was not the policeman who had to prove that you are under suspicion, but you had to prove to the policeman that you were not.

The Communists did everything they could so that everyone was under suspicion. This is why it was difficult to unite the people. Solidarity broke this.

In the mountains underground life was very active. People clung to old ways. They were themselves, and they did not change in relation to the church. They were true.

Now when they went to an office, when they had to deal with state clerks, lying was the normal thing. It is true that even today we have this inheritance from communism. But this habit of duplicity has to be broken. Fortunately it was not so strong here in the mountains. The internal pride of these people did not allow them to live in a lie.

For example, when their land was taken, people first went to lawyers. They could do nothing. Then they prayed. These prayers could not change things but they provided meaning. They reinforced the knowledge that these actions were illegal and that they hurt people. The

Jozef Tischner

church, which could not unwind the new rules, could still do a lot because it morally stood on the side of the people, and it gave them strength—which turned to power.

Also they believed that communism was not going to last. It was just a matter of time. And this helped people to be anti-Communist. So when Solidarity emerged, the solidarity of the farmers here in the mountains was already very strong. They organized and they started to fight for ownership of the land, not individually but together in an organization.

How did they fight? Did they physically try to take back the land?

The fight for land had two levels. On the one hand it meant talks with the government, with the ministry. A commission was formed. This was the legal struggle.

But on the other level it was extraordinary. One day, the mountain people, the highlanders defied the orders of the ministry and simply went to the mountains. They took their sheep and went to the mountains. It was an extraordinary moment. It was night when the shepherds reached the mountains with their sheep. Then, the sun began to rise and the highlanders simply went about their normal shepherd life—cleaning up, cutting the grass, as a beautiful dawn emerged. Spontaneously, they began singing beautiful mountain songs. The echo went all over the mountains. And the song came back to them. One of them told me that from some far away valley a voice could be heard, a voice of a woman, who cried, "Jesus Christ, the highlanders are back."

What did the authorities do?

When the shepherds went to the Tatra Mountains, the Communists did not answer with violence. They had other methods. They could levy fines, for example. If the fine was not paid, then they could take possessions away, like the house. These methods were widely used. They sent officials with certain documents, they summoned people to court.

It has to be remembered that the Communists had full authority in Poland. They were in power not only by police, not only by officials, but also by the distribution of goods, like coal. So, for example, the shepherds could not get permission to buy coal. Everything was in the hands of Communists, so you could say this revolt was like trying to commit suicide.

You were teaching at the university, and the Communists stopped you from doing that. Could you describe to me the paradox of teaching philosophy on the one hand and being interrogated by the secret police on the other hand?

The Communist times were full of paradoxes, and I don't really know whether to laugh at these paradoxes or to cry. These were tragic times, but also funny. Communism is very dangerous, but in Poland it was becoming weak. So, in practice, it sometimes looked rather silly. The secret police invited people to their so-called interviews.

Of course, these were not really invitations. They wanted the person being interviewed to feel that he was under suspicion, that he was guilty and that the police could catch him any time. And that the police knew everything. Sometimes these psychological activities impressed people. Sometimes they did not.

People got used to it but it wasn't nice.

The secret police particularly watched priests who were important socially. Because I was a teacher at the university, and a teacher of the clergy and also because I published a lot of work, I was a subject—or rather an object of interest to the police.

From time to time they invited me for an interview. For example I published an article in an underground illegal paper, and the secret police did not like that at all.

They warned me that this could have bad consequences for me. I also had many contacts with foreigners. I was interrogated by Mr. Pietruszka then, the one who was responsible for organizing the assault of Popieluszko. They told me that by going abroad I was leading an anti-socialist activity. I did not know what it meant, but I knew that many times just breathing and sleeping could be anti-socialist.

Once the police took my letters. And they started asking: Who is this? What is this? I was especially observed when I went to Gdansk to hold lectures. The police did not tell me not to go but they warned me not to say anything against the state. This sort of unnerved me because it was illegal. But I always knew that my activities were far more dangerous for communism than communism was for me. Still, it was not pleasant.

Is it possible that something positive might have been learned by any of you from the experience of communism.

Jozef Tischner

On the one hand communism has shown us how malicious evil can be, how lying and how two-faced. On the other hand, something has been proven, even under this system. Spirit cannot be killed, soul cannot be killed. A man can be hurt, but the soul cannot be killed. It is unreachable by these means.

One more question. The church in other countries has a poor record against communism. It was co-opted, it collaborated. But here in Poland where the church behaved well, relatively well and was strong against communism, here everyone's now worried about the power of the church, that it could push its way into civil laws as well as moral laws. Can you explain this paradox?

The situation is different in Warsaw than in Zakopane. I should emphasize that the church does not want power. The church has a power over a human being and the church knows what kind of power it has.

Each human being has a religious feeling. Each comes to church because of that, because of that religious feeling inside. Such is the nature of man. Even if he's not a Catholic, he will come to listen about the most basic of things, and this is our power. We don't want any other power.

But there is a problem. Elections are going to be held very soon. There are no political parties. We don't know whom to elect. People go to the priest and ask, please tell me whom shall I vote for. Not far away from here, for example, a hospital was started by the Communists and now there is no money to continue the construction. Everyone says let the church do it, let the church gather money. People trust the church. This is not the power we necessarily want, but if the church does not build this hospital, then the hospital is not going to exist.

Then there's the problem of education. Our education is bad. Our teachers are not well educated. But Catholic schools have emerged and these are popular, twenty people applying for each place. Because these are good schools. It is only the church that has the moral authority, and the good people to run these schools.

And that's how authority and power comes into the hands of the church. It is dangerous, but the church has not done these things to gain power.

What about the issue of abortion and the idea of Catholicism as a national religion?

Ah, the problem of the abortion law and the problem of religion at schools. They are very different. Until now we have had Communist laws concerning abortions. They are the worst in all Europe. I believe that after some discussion we will have a humanistic European law in this matter.

As far as school is concerned, school was a Communist institution. And the bringing up of children here has been based on Communist principles, which were in fact not bringing them up at all. So the issue of religion in schools is a matter of trying to cure the schools of the absolute void that was there before. It is not so dangerous as it might seem to you, an American. We will maybe have something like what is in Germany or Austria. Religion is there, available at school for people who want it.

There is only one problem really. What is the attitude of the church to democracy? That's the key to this question of the church's power. Can the Polish church help in building democracy? The Catholic church, as a whole, is not notable for building democracy. Very often democracy has been built in spite of the Catholic church.

But I think this has changed after the fall of communism, because two consecutive totalitarianisms—Hitlerism and communism—have opened the eyes of the church to the values of democracy. Democracy is now valued much more by the church than in the 19th Century.

This is truly the last question. Would you tell me your favorite mountain story?

OK, there was a man, a shepherd, sitting beside his house in the sun, and a friend comes by and asks, "What do you do when you have free time?"
"I sit and think," says the shepherd.
"And when you don't have free time?" asks the friend.
"Then I just sit."
That's how I am.

16

The Shepherd: We Want to Own This Land Again

What did the Communists want to do with your valley, your lands here, and what were you able to do about it?

The Communist government wanted to build Poland. They gave us fertilizers. And then, out of the blue, they just took everything away. And they took people away too. Somewhere—I don't know. They sort of took control over us. But now they see that they hurt us. There are a lot of forests here that belong to us. But they are still under state control. Many people went abroad. And many people come here from abroad. You're not the only people who have come here.

There was a lot of grass here. The sheep in my grandfather's time used to graze here and now everything is more expensive and nothing is better.

Andrzej Gal, a shepherd, has lived in the Tatra Mountains all his life. He was jailed for three months for refusing to give up his fields. In 1983, Pope John Paul II visited Mr. Gal at his shed in the Tatras.

We are still waiting but we don't know how long we'll last. No one is saving us. We want to own this land again.

Our ancestors fought for this land. We never sold this land to the government. We want them to give it back to us.

What does this land mean to you and what did the Communists want to do with the land?

This land was everything for us. We need it to graze the sheep and the cows. The Communists wanted to fight against the people here, the Highlanders. They wanted to devastate us. The Communists still exist, somewhere. We are still sitting here. The price of wool is not going up. How can we live? You in America, you have prosperity. You have a different government. You have discipline and culture.

What about us? We have no coal. There is not enough wood to burn. We have to have money and where do we get the money from? From the cheese, perhaps, but from nothing else. That's the truth. We are going to wait this one year and maybe if nothing improves we're going to just go abroad.

When the Communists tried to take away your land, what did you do about it? Did you ever try to get it back, and did you ever get in trouble with the Communists?

Yes, we fought for it and we're still fighting for it. It is not over. But we don't know how to do it. We don't have any weapons to fight with. What can we do? We write. One minister gives promises, another one does, but nothing happens. And no minister wants to give it back. Nobody wants to give it back to us.

If there were more people, if there were other shepherds here, maybe we could say something more interesting. They forced us out of these lands. All these sheds were full of shepherds and full of sheep, two thousand sheep.

I was imprisoned for it. Three months. I was imprisoned for three months by the Communist government because I didn't want to leave this field. Then I settled with a lawyer, and I think I signed a paper or something, I don't know. What else do you want me to say? I graze sheep. That's all. There's nothing else to say.

Andrzej Gal

Are you a Christian, and has the church in any way helped you in any of this?

Yes, it did help. I am a Christian. I prayed, and God is very important. I believe in God, I go to church. I know all the church ceremonies.

The Pope was here in 1983 in our cottage, and he gave us something and we served him some food. We had some friends here, but we couldn't do much. Because we didn't know that he was coming. At those times, nobody told us that he was coming to visit us, but somehow we managed to welcome him. But we were afraid then because we didn't know who was coming and at the very last moment they told us that the Pope was about to visit us. Things happened like that then.

But now everything is beautiful and great. Times are much better, and maybe this year he will visit us again. I feel sorry that our times are the way they are, but we can manage.

We don't know what's happening. They hold our hands, our legs. You know we had bad times with the Germans and the French, but still we can't do anything. We can't figure out our situation. That's how it goes, in Poland.

III

The German Antecedent

Eberhard Bethge

Professor Bethge and the Bonhoeffer Legacy

What happened to the Protestant church in Germany in 1933 and 1934?

For the majority of Germans, 1933 was, of course, a year of great hope, because after the Weimar Republic, after the defeat of the First World War and the Versailles Treaty, everybody looked for someone who would repair the status of Germany, and would make it respectable in the world again. And they hoped Hitler would do it.

And Hitler did something, actually, when he left the League of Nations, because Germany was not equal to the other nations. Everybody hailed him. The pastors, the churches, the church governments, they hailed him for that. And I as a young student in those years, I thought Hitler was doing right, politically.

Dr. Eberhard Bethge was a close friend of the German theologian, Dietrich Bonhoeffer. Bonhoeffer's struggle with the predicament of attempting to live as a Christian in Nazi Germany has provided the moral vocabulary for understanding the conflict between totalitarianism, civic action and the individual conscience in later generations. Bonhoeffer was executed by the Nazis on April 9, 1945. Dr. Bethge, who was imprisoned during the War, now lives with his wife Renate, Bonhoeffer's niece, in Wachtberg-Villiprott, Germany.

We didn't really see the point of the anti-Semitism in Hitler's doctrines, and so we said, oh, that's not important, the politics he makes, that's important. He makes us respectable in the world. Consequently, most of the churches said, now, we must go with him. And even people who later opposed him tried to distinguish between Hitler the politician and the second or third row of people who tried to do what Hitler had written in *Mein Kampf,* his book of the '20s.

We hadn't read that book, of course, we didn't take it seriously. We thought his politics were all right, and we were maybe on his side until he tried to put the Protestant church into the hands of men who were Nazis.

They claimed to be Christians. And they tried to marry Christianity and Naziism. The first opposition to them came about in the summer of '33. They lost the church elections, which Hitler had ordered to take place. They wanted to forbid people of Jewish descent from holding any office in the church.

They said, if there was a pastor whose grandmother was Jewish, he shouldn't preach. We said no, that is impossible. The church is not just Germany, the church is the body of Christ, and you enter the church by baptism and not by having Aryan blood.

But they even tried to prove that Christ was not a Jew, but that he was an Aryan because he was brought up in Galilee, and they found some evidence that there were not only Semites but certain Aryan families there too. This was changing, of course, the whole doctrine of the church. Some said it might be true. There is certain evidence in the New Testament of how anti-Jewish Jesus actually behaved. Some professors supported that doctrine with very, very exact research.

So we had certain professors even in Berlin, who went that way. They said that those who still emphasized the Jewishness of Christianity could not lead the church. They mixed up Christianity with Aryanism and that created fights in the seminaries and fights in the ministries.

Whom were you actually fighting in '33?

It was clear that Hitler himself and some of his backers just didn't know any better. But the other ones in the church government or at the theological faculties, teachers of theology who tried to combine German-ism and Christianity, those we had to fight. We considered them first of all our enemies and the enemies of the true church. But still we

Eberhard Bethge

differentiated between this fight in religious matters and the fight in political matters.

I was a young man, coming from the country and I and the group to which I belonged tried for two or three years to see a difference between fighting Nazism politically, which I didn't do, and fighting Nazis or half-Nazi church people who we saw as betrayers of the Christian faith.

Could you explain the historic context within the church of the concept of Aryanization?

There, of course, is an old tradition of this in Germany. Martin Luther was very anti-Jewish when he realized that they wouldn't convert to Christianity. We had learned that from the beginning, or you might say inherited it. It was a matter of course to think that way. And there is also the even older tradition of French and English and Germanic philosophers in the last century who said that there is a danger in the mixture of clean, Nordic blood and philosophy with Jewish elements, which will destroy the real power of intellect and the physical power and then the political power of the Nordic race.

We were anti-Jewish, anti-Semitic, and we thought this was Christian. And remember we felt that Germany had been stabbed in the back in the First World War. And the guilty people were Bolsheviks and Jewish people from the East or from Russia.

These were the real enemies. We felt we had to fight the Jews, politically, and bring them down from their great places of influence in cultural work, in the theater, in music, in administration, in banking and all that. This was a very popular in Germany, of course.

And so in 1933, the point was made that the church, too, must co-fight with the Nazis to eliminate Jewish influence, even in the church. We were allowed to preach as we have preached all along, but we had to accept this cleansing of the Jewish influence in the church.

Some believed more in it, some less, and some mistrusted it. Only a very few saw the point. One of those very few was, of course, Deitrich Bonhoeffer who already on the 15th of April, 1933 had finished an article in which he said that this issue of the Aryan clauses was such a point of principle that even if it touches only a small number of people in the church—which was the case—we must deny it.

What were these Aryan clauses?

In the beginning of April, 1933, the Nazis introduced legislation which said all people of Jewish descent were not allowed any more to be employees of the state or civil servants. That included people in government, even professors at universities, because in Germany all universities are state universities, and even theological professors are employees of the state.

About that same week, there was the first huge rally of the Nazi Christians of the Protestant church in Berlin. They proclaimed that we must have the same law in the church as well. The fight went on for three or four months.

At the beginning of September, 1933, the church in Berlin and of the northern area of the country held a synod and declared that they would introduce the Aryan clause into church legislation. And that was the point when the opposition said, no. This is impossible. Then the opposition was rather small. They were a minority, but they said we will fight that.

Tell me more about the majority. Who were they? How did they feel?

They were not people in the government. Suddenly many other people discovered that they had such a deep Aryan inner feeling that they couldn't bear to sit next to a Jew. And that a Jew had a different way of behaving, a different way of thinking, he has a different way of doing everything. This was, of course, very bad.

And so the feeling was that we Germans must clean—in the very clear sense of the word clean—the atmosphere which was gathering this kind of poison, Jewish poison.

"Bad blood" was the great term. You had to have Aryan blood. Jewish blood was itself already a mixture of bad blood which makes bad character and tries to govern by power, by violence and to push down the Germans.

So we know this Jewish poison had to be cleansed. How did they propose to do that? What was this clause?

For instance, everybody in an office, in a village, in a city, in a province, in Berlin, had to prove that he had Aryan ancestors. How could he do that? He could do it only if he wrote to church officers in the villages or

Eberhard Bethge

in the cities and asked them to look in the old books of the church in which baptisms were recorded.

So many pastors and church secretaries had to work for hours and hours, weeks and months to answer all these requests. "Please give me an excerpt out of the church files that proves my ancestors had been Christians."

The church officers and the ministers, they didn't care. They did that. They said, "How important we are now." I was an assistant curator in the winter of '33. I had to sit all morning and look through the books and answer these letters.

How did the church respond to this situation?

The church didn't know how to react. It called for its experts to write papers about what it might mean to Aryanize the church. And a few people wrote statements, which we have published already, that basically said, "Let's take it seriously. What does this renewal mean? Maybe it is a very good idea." And some very few said sharply, "This actually is the destruction of the inner rule and the strength and the authenticity of the Christian faith."

Please explain, for those who don't know, who Dietrich Bonhoeffer was?

Dietrich Bonhoeffer was a twin, the fifth or sixth child of a wealthy Berlin family. The son of a medical doctor, a professor of psychiatry and neurology. Dietrich studied theology, and had just started his career as a lecturer as assistant professor at Berlin University. From the very beginning, he was quite clear about the deadly danger for the church of this doctrine being accepted.

Of course, he was a very young man and nobody knew him really. In April, 1933, he sat down and wrote an article, now rather famous, about the church and the Jewish question. It was very clear, but it was published in a little magazine and nobody took it very seriously. He argued that Aryanism—the issue of asking what blood one has in one's veins— destroyed baptism as the door to the church.

In July, 1933, there were church elections all over Germany. There was on the one side the party of so-called German Christians, these were Nazi Germans. Many were people who thought they were really Christians but wanted to be Germans as well. They were the majority, about 72%. The rest voted for the other side who said we cannot introduce this new doctrine into the church.

You were a friend of Dietrich Bonhoeffer?

In '33 I was a country boy. I was theologically educated there and I wanted to be ordained there. In April, 1935, I was already a member of the so-called Confessing Church, the opposition. I was sent to one of the Confessing Church seminaries to prepare for ordination. The director was a young man named Dietrich Bonhoeffer.

I had not heard of him. I was not a Berliner. He was only three years older than I was, a sporty man smoking a cigarette when I first met him. I knew nothing about the article he had written against the Aryan clause in the church.

The Nazis, of course, were aware of how important was the question of who will be a pastor. Will you greet the congregation with a "heil Hitler," and with a military spirit which would have an influence on the children. Or, if you had studied the Gospels well, you were an interpreter of the real gospel. This was the great fight between the true church and of the wrong church in those days.

Soon the opposition came to the point that they had to ask young people not to go to the universities, but to go to the "emergency institutes" of the Confessing Church. Dietrich was the director of the institute that I attended in 1935. He came from a liberal Protestant family in which Martin Luther was highly regarded, but in which Enlightenment philosophy was welded together with Christian belief.

He knew as a young boy the world of Berlin, theaters, philosophy, music. Yet even before 1933, he was dissatisfied with the way the church behaved. It had become much too liberal, much too nationalistic-minded, and many of its professors had lost the very center of Christian faith. He was influenced by the Christ-centered theology of Karl Barth who had come as a professor to Bonn from Switzerland.

We might have become Nazis in '33, but there was our young teacher, Dietrich Bonhoeffer, who gave us an absolutely different picture of what Germany could be. What the church could be. What politics should be and of what Christian doctrine should be. From the very beginning he was very clear that we had to stand for Christ and even for the Jews — the brothers and sisters of Jesus.

Eberhard Bethge

He sometimes said that 1935 and the next years were the happiest time of his life, preparing young members of the opposition to live as Christians, in a Christian way, by serving the true church in Nazi Germany.

I remember that some friends of his came to our seminar one day to talk about emigration to Britain. They had fallen under the Aryan clause, and for me, a country boy from the province, it was the first time I had met any of the victims of that legislation. That changed the whole issue for me when I saw what they had to suffer.

Tell about Dietrich Bonhoeffer's role in the conspiracy to kill Hitler?

Dietrich Bonhoeffer considered first his duty to be a man of the church, and to try to influence faculties and church people to become clear in church matters. For years he considered whether he should become politically engaged. In 1939, he contemplated going to America and becoming a teacher there. He was wanted in the United States. He was not wanted in Germany. By 1938 he knew about actual preparations for a conspiracy to stop Hitler. His brothers and brother-in-law were active in it.

He was from the very beginning in resistance by not conforming to the way Nazi Germans or Hitler wanted Christians to go. But after a time official opposition was no longer possible. At that point it became clear that this fatal government could only be stopped by a putsch, by an overthrow, by stopping Hitler by any means.

Dietrich understood this. He belonged to the faction in the opposition which saw clearly that the only way was to kill Hitler. He believed that he had to accept the guilt of killing the head of state in order to stop the much greater guilt of the killing of the Jews.

How did he approach this theologically?

Dietrich Bonhoeffer had been a passivist since the beginning of the '30s. He felt that the military spirit even in the church was a great evil. But then Hitler began killing the Jews. After that to say "I don't want to take a weapon, a pistol or machine gun," was privately very respectable. But I you chose that path, you avoided your responsibility to your fellow citizens, the Jews.

In 1939, Bonhoeffer went to America, where he was invited by Henry Smith Leiper of the Federal Council of Churches to stay and assist with the settlement of German emigrants in New York. He declined the invitation. "I must live through this difficult period of our national history with the Christians of Germany. I shall have no right to take part in the restoration of Christian life in Germany after the war unless I share the trials of this time with my people," he wrote in a letter to theologian Reinhold Niebuhr in June of that year.

So that very Christian peaceful spirit became the weapon against you. Do you understand what that means? This is the greatness of Dietrich Bonhoeffer. He would not fanatically say, "I want to be a pacifist in all circumstances." The guilt of sitting there silent and not speaking out and not acting to stop Hitler's Auschwitz policies, that was a real guilt. And the guilt you had to take on for killing was Hitler comparatively really nothing.

I remember sitting in a room with Dietrich and some others in the early '40s. Hans Dohnanyi, his brother-in-law, who was very central in the conspiracy preparations asked Dietrich about the Gospels. He was a layman. "There is that sentence in the Bible, 'whoever takes a sword will perish by the sword.' What about us?"

Dietrich said, "It is exactly the people who accept the validity of that saying—he who lives by the sword will die by the sword—exactly these people are needed now in the conspiracy."

He knew that he was not guiltless even in an emergency situation. But to avoid acting would be participating in endless and unforgivable guilt.

When you read Dietrich Bonhoeffer's letters now carefully, the ones smuggled to his parents from the military prison, you know that there was ambivalence in his heart. He wanted to live. He was a strong human being, and he had all the wishes of the physical life. He was working to survive.

At the same time, he knew that by compromising, he would mean nothing in the future. And now, as you can see, he means something. Dietrich Bonhoeffer is one of the few Germans who is being heard and listened to. But it's because he accepted the final consequence.

How did he die?

He was in prison about two years. He was imprisoned on the 5th of April 1943. The Gestapo had some suspicions that there was a group working against Hitler. But they had no proof. In prison he was allowed visitors—his wife, his parents and sometimes I saw him when I was on vacation in Berlin. He worked there. His cell was a study.

After the failure of the plot to kill Hitler of the 20th of July, 1944, documents were discovered naming all the people involved. He was removed from military prison and taken to the Gestapo basement prison at the headquarters on Prinz Albrecht Strasse.

Eberhard Bethge

He was then brought to the concentration camp at Buchenwald in February of 1945 and then moved to the Flossenberg camp near the Czechoslovakian border and there on the 9th of April 1945 he was hanged after a night's court martial meeting at Gestapo headquarters in Berlin.

By then I was in prison myself.

FAITH UNDER FIRE

Designed by Augustin Hedberg

Composed at The Lawrenceville School
Publications Department
Type: Adobe Garamond using PageMaker
on the Apple Macintosh IICX system.

Cover design and photograph of the
domes of the Klokoty Monastery
in southern Bohemia by
Sheldon Sturges.